OSPREY AIRCRAFT OF THE ACES • 91

Brewster F2A Buffalo
Aces of World War 2

SERIES EDITOR: TONY HOLMES

OSPREY AIRCRAFT OF THE ACES • 91

Brewster F2A Buffalo Aces of World War 2

Kari Stenman and Andrew Thomas

OSPREY
PUBLISHING

Front cover
On the morning of 13 December 1941, British and Commonwealth forces in northern Malaya were reeling from the ferocity of the Japanese invasion that had been launched less than a week earlier. The harbour on Penang Island, off Malaya's west coast, had been heavily attacked in previous days, so at 0600 hrs the first three of sixteen Buffaloes from No 453 Sqn Royal Australian Air Force (RAAF) left Ipoh for Butterworth as reinforcements for the hard pressed fighters that were trying to defend the area. Flying AN185/TD-V, Flt Lt Doug Vanderfield led Sgts Bill Collyer and Mal Read ahead of the rest of the unit.

No sooner had they landed at Butterworth than they were ordered off to intercept another raid on Penang. Some 18 Ki-48 'Lily' twin-engined bombers of the Japanese Army Air Force's 75th and 90th Sentais had been sent to attack the town, these machines being identified as 'Mitsubishis' by British soldiers. Just prior to the Ki-48s arriving overhead Penang, three Ki-51 'Sonias' (reported as 'Stukas') of the 59th Sentai began attacking shipping in the nearby harbour.

The Buffaloes immediately took off again, climbing up into cloud cover before diving on the intruders. Following his leader, Bill Collyer recounted;

'Vanderfield was having problems with his undercarriage. His wheels were still down. Read and I were in line astern. At about 7000 ft Vanderfield led an attack on a "Betty". The port engine caught fire and the aircraft dived into the sea. No one bailed out.'

Collyer had just described future Buffalo ace Vanderfield's first victory against the Axis powers. The latter also recalled the action;

'We immediately took off and intercepted three Japanese bombers. We attacked these bombers, and five or six dive-bombers then came out of the clouds and attacked us. We let them have the works and definitely shot down two in the first attack. A sergeant pilot in my flight fired on a dive-bomber that was trying to sit on my tail, and it rolled over and disappeared. Another went out to sea in a long dive.'

First published in Great Britain in 2010 by Osprey Publishing
Midland House, West Way, Botley, Oxford, OX2 0PH
443 Park Avenue South, New York, NY, 10016, USA
E-mail: info@ospreypublishing.com

ISBN: 978 1 84603 481 7
E-book ISBN: 978 1 84908 249 5

Edited by Tony Holmes
Page design by Tony Truscott
Cover Artwork by Mark Postlethwaite
Aircraft Profiles by Chris Davey
Scale Drawings by Mark Styling
Index by Michael Forder
Printed and bound in China through Bookbuilders

09 10 11 12 13   10 9 8 7 6 5 4 3 2 1

FOR A CATALOGUE OF ALL BOOKS PUBLISHED BY OSPREY MILITARY AND AVIATION PLEASE CONTACT:

Osprey Direct, c/o Random House Distribution Center,
400 Hahn Road, Westminster, MD 21157
Email: uscustomerservice@ospreypublishing.com

Osprey Direct, The Book Service Ltd, Distribution Centre,
Colchester Road, Frating Green, Colchester, Essex, CO7 7DW
E-mail: customerservice@ospreypublishing.com

www.ospreypublishing.com

Collyer and Read were also successful, the pair sharing in the destruction of a Ki-51, whilst the latter was also credited with two more 'Sonias' destroyed. By now short of fuel, the Buffaloes had to land almost immediately. Ground observers reported that three enemy aircraft had indeed come down, whilst a fourth had staggered away trailing black smoke. With Butterworth under attack, Vanderfield headed directly back to Ipoh. His two wingmen landed briefly at Butterworth, however, before heading back to Ipoh as well.

After landing, Doug Vanderfield was credited with two of the twin-engined bombers and one dive-bomber destroyed, thus setting him on the path to 'acedom'. He achieved this accolade on 17 January 1942, becoming one of only four Allied pilots to attain this highly coveted status whilst flying the Buffalo. More remarkably, he had achieved his first three victories with his aircraft's undercarriage stuck down! (*Cover artwork by Mark Postlethwaite*)

CONTENTS

CHAPTER ONE

THE 'PEANUT SPECIAL' 6

CHAPTER TWO

BREWSTERS OVER KARELIA 10

CHAPTER THREE

FINNISH STALEMATE 21

CHAPTER FOUR

OVER THE GULF OF FINLAND 28

CHAPTER FIVE

MALAYAN CAMPAIGN 42

CHAPTER SIX

DEFENDERS OF BURMA 68

CHAPTER SEVEN

FINALE OVER LAND AND SEA 78

APPENDICES 85
COLOUR PLATES COMMENTARY 91
BIBLIOGRAPHY 95
INDEX 96

THE 'PEANUT SPECIAL'

The Brewster Buffalo, which was to gain an unenviable record for inadequacy and mediocrity in World War 2, had its origins in a 1935 requirement for a new generation carrier fighter for the US Navy. Amongst others, the required capabilities included that it be a monoplane with an enclosed cockpit, retractable undercarriage, wing flaps and an integral arrestor hook for carrier operations. The Brewster Aeronautical Corporation submitted Model 39 as its proposal, the aircraft being designed around the 950 hp Wright XR-1820-22 radial engine. The fighter was initially fitted with just two 0.50-in machine guns above the engine, although its firepower was later doubled when two more weapons of an identical size were installed in the wings.

Brewster's Model 39 was designated the F2A by the US Navy, and prototype XF2A-1 BuNo 0451 first flew from Brewster's Long Island facility on 2 December 1937. Development testing by the company continued into 1938, and on 11 June resulted in the US Navy's Bureau of Aeronautics placing a production order for 54 F2A-1s, so assuring its place in history as the US Navy's first operational monoplane fighter. Production aircraft were fitted with the R-1820-34 engine of 940 hp, and following wind tunnel tests their fins were enlarged. After further modifications, the fighter's initially disappointing performance was increased to give the F2A a top speed of 300+ mph at 17,000 ft.

A developed variant, designated the F2A-2, was ordered on 22 March 1939. The original prototype was suitably modified to this standard through the fitment of a 1200 hp Wright R-1820-40 Cyclone engine, which boasted an improved carburettor. The F2A-2 also featured a more effective rudder. Testing of the XF2A-2 began in July, and the aircraft soon demonstrated a marked increase in performance that saw it capable of achieving a maximum speed of 340 mph in level flight. Production examples of the F2A-2 began entering frontline service the following year. Finally, the US Navy ordered a total of 108 F2A-3s in January 1941, but the weight associated with its increased armoured protection and improved equipment adversely affected the fighter's already modest performance.

The first fighter squadron to be equipped with the F2A-1 was Lt Cdr Warren Harvey's VF-3, which was assigned to the air group embarked in USS *Saratoga* (CV-3). This unit

The Brewster XF2A-1 prototype is seen here on an early test flight, this retouched contemporary photograph revealing its distinctive barrel-like fuselage and the original low-profile cockpit and small fin (*Peter Mersky*)

accepted its first examples on 8 December 1939, VF-3 eventually receiving ten of the eleven F2A-1s issued to the US Navy – it operated them alongside nine F3F-1 biplanes. The remaining 43 F2A-1s built by Brewster were sold to Finland as B-239s in 1940 (see Chapter 2). An identical number of F2A-2s were ordered in their place, while eight of the original F2A-1s were remanufactured as F2A-2s.

Among VF-3's pilots at this time were future aces Lt John S 'Jimmy' Thach and Ens Edward H 'Butch' O'Hare. The latter made his first F2A-1 flight on 26 July 1940, commenting after his first carrier deck landing in the type that it was 'just about the most exciting thing a pilot can do in peacetime'. Thach later became the unit's CO.

The next unit to fly the F2A was VF-2, which was entirely manned by non-commissioned chief petty officer pilots. It had received 18 F2A-2s by November 1940, and it took them aboard USS *Lexington* (CV-2) in March 1941 for a training cruise to Hawaii. By the following September VF-2 had transitioned to the F2A-3.

Despite the aircraft's introduction to fleet service, engine unreliability continued to dog the fighter – bearing problems necessitated frequent overhauls. The landing gear failures that had plagued the F2A-1 also persisted with the F2A-2, and despite repeated attempts by Brewster to cure these problems, they were never completely eliminated. Nevertheless, US Navy pilots were generally pleased with the improved F2A-2s, and most regarded them with some affection. Indeed, the portly Brewsters were nicknamed 'Peanut Specials' in fleet service. Both VF-2 and VF-3 re-equipped with the more robust Grumman F4F Wildcat within weeks of the outbreak of the war with Japan, however, and their F2A-2/3s were passed on to the US Marine Corps.

Brewster had delivered just 162 aircraft to the US Navy, although a further 346 examples were built for export.

— EUROPEAN EXPORTS —

Faced with a rapidly deteriorating political situation in Europe in the late 1930s, many western governments looked to the USA for equipment as they tried to counter the threat posed by a resurgent Nazi Germany. One such country was Belgium, which persuaded the US government to allow Brewster

The US Navy's first monoplane fighter squadron was VF-3, whose F2A-1s were assigned to the air group embarked in USS Saratoga (CV-3). BuNo 1393 '3-F-13' had a minor landing mishap on 19 March 1940 whilst being flown by future ace Lt Jimmy Thach. Quickly repaired, the fighter was also flown later that year by another future ace, and Medal of Honour recipient, Lt(jg) 'Butch' O'Hare (US Navy)

The only other US Navy fighter unit to fly the F2A was VF-2, embarked in USS Lexington (CV-2), which was manned by non-commissioned chief petty officer pilots. VF-2's F2A-2 BuNo 1412 '2-F-7' was photographed in flight in late 1940. The unit transitioned to the F4F soon after the start of the Pacific War (US Navy)

to develop and build a land-based equivalent of the F2A-2 ahead of the aircraft on order for the US Navy aircraft. Designated the B-339B, some 40 fighters were ordered, but only one had reached France by the time Germany launched its *Blitzkrieg* in the west on 10 May 1940. Six more B-339Bs ended up on the Caribbean island of Martinique under French control, where they languished.

The Dutch too were on the lookout for additional fighters to equip the fighter units of the Royal Netherlands Indies Army Air Corps (ML-KNIL) in an effort to counter

The F2A attracted considerable export interest, and one of the fighter's early customers was Belgium, which acquired 40 aircraft. The F2A was redesignated the B-339B in Belgian service, and the first example completed by Brewster bore the US civil registration NX56B (the 56th F2A built and 'B' for Belgium) during flight testing with the manufacturer (*Peter Mersky*)

possible Japanese expansion in the Far East. In late 1939 they also ordered the Brewster fighter, purchasing 72 fighters as the B-339C/D. Later, a further 20 B-439s (identical to the US Navy's F2A-3) were ordered as well, although these were ultimately delivered to Australia following the fall of the East Indies in early 1942.

Britain also eyed the US as a potential source of war materiel, and in 1939 the British Purchasing Commission decided to place an order for 170 B-339Es, naming the type Buffalo. By any standard the performance of the portly machine fell well below that of the latest contemporary British and German fighters, and after testing early examples in the UK they were deemed to be unsuitable for service in Western Europe. Thus, almost all of the British order was diverted to equip fighter squadrons forming in the Far East.

However, the balance of the Belgian contract was delivered to Britain, where, in September 1940, US volunteer pilots serving in the RAF had assembled at Church Fenton to form No 71 'Eagle' Sqn. At the end of the month seven-victory ace Sqn Ldr Walter Churchill arrived as CO, with fellow ace Flt Lt Royce Wilkinson as one of his flight commanders. The new unit eagerly awaited some aircraft, and its pilots were somewhat disappointed when, on 24 October, three Buffaloes were delivered – a somewhat unkind gesture by Fighter Command, as many of the Americans had previously been flying Spitfires! Soon afterwards Walter Churchill wrote, 'It is strongly recommended that this type should on no account be considered as a fighter without considerable modification'. However, he also commented, 'As a trainer the aircraft is delightful. It behaves with the ease of a Gladiator and is just as simple to aerobat. So far we have found no vices'.

The Buffaloes did not last long with the 'Eagles' as four days later Plt Off Phil Leckrone turned one over on landing and, on 3 November, Churchill had an alarming experience when one of the inspection panels in the tail opened in flight, making the aircraft very difficult to control. He managed to get down at Linton-on-Ouse. Upon his return to Church Fenton Churchill was informed that the unit was to be re-equipped with Hurricane Is – the first nine arrived from No 85 Sqn four days later.

With the RAF unenthusiastic about the Buffalo, the ex-Belgian aircraft were passed on to the Royal Navy instead. Some were issued to training units, but 12 were sent to the Mediterranean, where, in January 1941, they partially equipped newly-formed 805 Naval Air Squadron (NAS) at Aboukir, in Egypt. The following month at least one of the Buffaloes embarked alongside some Fulmar Is aboard HMS *Eagle*.

On 6 March 805 NAS's CO, Lt Cdr Alan Black, led a detachment of six Fulmar Is and three Buffaloes (AS419, AS420 and AX814) to Maleme, in western Crete, for the defence of the anchorage at nearby Suda Bay. The Buffalo flight was led by Lt Rupert Brabner, who had previously been the Member of Parliament for Hythe. On the 19th, he was scrambled in AS419 when some Italian bombers were spotted heading for the island, although his Buffalo developed engine trouble before he reached them so he returned to Maleme. A total loss of power on his final approach caused Brabner to land short of the runway and the Buffalo overturned. Luckily, the fighter's anti-roll bar worked and the MP escaped unharmed. Brabner later achieved 'acedom' during the epic convoy battles of 1942.

Among 805 NAS's pilots at this time was Sub Lt John Sykes, who recalled to the authors especially for this volume that 'Rupert Brabner was a splendid man – he had been an MP and was very cultured and intelligent, as well as being a damned fine fighter pilot. The Buffalo was a delight to fly, as it was very manoeuvrable and particularly light on the controls'.

Brabner's was thought to have been the only operational Buffalo mission flown from Crete, although patrols in defence of the port of Alexandria continued from Egypt. During one such sortie over Royal Navy warships off Sidi Barrani on 17 June, Lt Lloyd Keith (who had five claims to his name, including three destroyed) was flying Buffalo AX813 when he was attacked and shot down by a Bf 109E from I./JG 27 flown by Oberfeldwebel Hermann Forster. The 26-year-old Canadian managed to crash-land and was taken prisoner, although he had been severely wounded in the action and died soon afterwards – the first Allied Buffalo pilot lost to enemy action.

805 NAS's Buffaloes were finally withdrawn in August after they had been replaced by Martlets that had initially been destined for service with the Greeks.

The Buffalo would soon see much more action, however, and meet with considerable success over the lakes and forests of Finland. It would experience a torrid time in the humid skies above the jungles of Malaya and Burma though in a combat career that lasted little more than two months.

Most of the ex-Belgian aircraft were transferred to the Royal Navy, and a number served operationally in the Mediterranean with 805 NAS's detachment on Crete. Among them was AS419, which was scrambled to intercept Italian bombers on 19 March 1941 but suffered an engine failure and turned over at Maleme airfield when the pilot attempted an emergency landing (*D H Coates*)

AS419's pilot, Lt Rupert Brabner, was uninjured in the crash. Formerly the MP for Hythe, he had experienced an abortive intercept of a Ju 88 the previous day. Brabner claimed his first victory (in a Fulmar) during the fighting over Crete, and subsequently became an ace during the Mediterranean convoy battles of 1942 (*via C F Shores*)

BREWSTERS OVER KARELIA

I n April 1939 the Finnish government contacted the Roosevelt administration in the USA as part of its search to hastily acquire modern combat aircraft for its air force. However, it was not until 17 October that same year that the Finnish Embassy in Washington, DC received a telegram clearing the purchase of fighter aircraft. Prompt availability, and compatibility with 87-octane fuel, were the only requirements stipulated by the Finns, and on 16 December a contract was signed with Brewster for the provision of 44 Model 239 fighters powered by the export-cleared 950 hp R-1820-G5 Cyclone engine. The total price to be paid was US$3.4 million, and the deal included the provision of spare parts, ten replacement engines and 20 Hamilton Standard propellers.

The fighters, which were approaching completion on the production line when the contract was signed, were to be delivered fully equipped, but with all US Navy equipment (including instruments, weapons and gunsights) removed.

The relevance of this purchase was starkly revealed on 30 November 1939 when the USSR invaded Finland following the cancellation of its non-aggression pact with the country 48 hours earlier. The Finnish Air Force was opposed by some 3253 Soviet aircraft at the start of the Winter War, so the new Brewster fighters were desperately needed. Built in four batches, they were crated up and loaded aboard a quartet of merchant

Experienced pilots from LLv 24 were posted to Sweden to collect the Brewster Model 239s that had recently arrived by sea from the USA. The aircraft were assembled by SAAB at Trollhättan, near Gothenburg, prior to being flown to Finland. The pilots are, from left to right, Viktor Pyötsiä, Eino Luukkanen, Yrjö Turkka, Jorma Karhunen and Jorma Sarvanto. Behind them is BW-384, which was flown to Finland on 11 April 1940. All bar Luukkanen were already aces from the Winter War (*J Sarvanto*)

ships in New York. The first vessel left the USA bound for Bergen, in Norway, on 13 January, followed one week later by a second shipment. The remaining aircraft were shipped on 7 and 19 February 1940.

Following their two-week voyage, the crates were sent by rail to Sweden, where the aircraft were reassembled at the SAAB facility at Trollhättan, near Gothenburg. Robert Winston of Brewster acted as test pilot for the new machines on site, and he performed the first flight of a Model 239 in European skies on 14 February. Finnish Air Force serials BW-351 to -394 were applied to the rear fuselage and undersurfaces of the wings following reassembly. The first four aircraft arrived in Finland on 1 March and the last of the Brewster 239s departed Sweden on 1 May.

The Winter War was in its final stages when the first Brewsters arrived in-country, and they were issued to newly formed squadron *Lentolaivue* (LLv) 22. The fighter flew a handful of uneventful interception missions before the Moscow peace treaty of 13 March 1940 ended hostilities. Five weeks later the Brewsters were transferred to LLv 24, which had initially been chosen to receive the first examples to reach Finland. However, in the critical last weeks of the Winter War the Fokker D.XXI-equipped unit could not be spared from operations to make the switch. LLv 24 initially flew the Model 239s from Malmi, near Helsinki, until its new base at Vesivehmaa, midway between Lahti and Heinola, became available in August 1940. The Brewsters would serve with LLv 24 until May 1944.

ACTION OVER KARELIA

On 22 June 1941 Germany launched its invasion of the USSR, codenamed Operation *Barbarossa*. The plans for this attack had been revealed to Finnish military leaders some four weeks earlier, allowing the Finns to mobilise their armed forces on 18 June in preparation for recovering the territory it had lost the previous year.

The 125 fighters of the Finnish Air Force were organised into two aviation regiments, namely *Lentorykmentti* (LeR) 2, commanded by Col Richard Lorentz, and LeR 3, led by Lt Col Einar Nuotio. LeR 2 controlled three fighter squadrons, with LLv 24 equipped with Brewster Model 239s, LLv 26 flying Italian-built Fiat G.50s and LLv 28 assigned French Morane-Saulnier MS.406s.

As of 25 June 1941, LLv 24 was led by Maj Gustaf Magnusson at Vesivehmaa. The nine fighters assigned to the unit's 1st Flight (commanded by Capt Eino Luukkanen) were also based here, as were the eight Brewsters of the 3rd Flight (led by 1Lt Jorma Karhunen) and the eight of the 4th Flight (with ace 1Lt Per Sovelius as flight leader). LLv 24's 2rd Flight (led by Capt Leo Ahola), equipped with eight Model 239s, was based at Selänpää.

At 0600 hrs on 25 June, the first Soviet bomber formations were spotted entering Finnish airspace near Turku. This news also reached nearby Selänpää, where 2/LLv 24 was located in case the squadron's main base at Vesivehmaa was the target of a surprise attack. The first pair of Brewsters took off at 0710 hrs and quickly engaged Soviet SB bombers, as future ace Cpl Heimo Lampi, piloting BW-354, recalled;

'Five minutes after take-off I observed a large formation of enemy aircraft. I attacked the bomber on the extreme right and set it on fire with my first burst. The aircraft went into a vertical dive and crashed into a forest. I then fired at two bombers on the right side of a three-aeroplane formation. One of the aircraft began to trail smoke and lose altitude. Chasing after it, the bomber slowed up so much that I had to pull away to the right to avoid a collision. This allowed its rear gunner to fire at me from very close range, although his aim was poor. Having dropped a little way behind my target, I turned back in behind its tail once more and hit the bomber's port engine with a short burst. Now trailing flames as well as smoke, the aircraft dived into the water.

'I saw SSgt Kinnunen down two aircraft during the same engagement.'

The intruders encountered by Lampi and Kinnunen were 27 SBs from 201st SBAP (high-speed bomber air regiment), which they had intercepted at a height of 1500 metres as the bombers approached Heinola. The Soviet crews were searching for LLv 24's main base at nearby Vesivehmaa, and five SBs were shot down by the two Brewster pilots.

Subsequent attacks were also repelled by LLv 24, and by dusk on 25 June the unit had flown a total of 77 sorties. The Soviet air force lost ten SBs in the unit's sector on this date, four of which were flown by squadron commanders – these losses have all been recently confirmed by records discovered in the Russian archives. Two aces had also been created on the 25th. SSgt Eero Kinnunen, in BW-352, claimed four and one shared bombers destroyed in two missions, thus raising his tally to eight, as he had been credited with three and one shared flying the D.XXI with LLv 24 in the Winter War. WO Yrjö Turkka, who had scored four and one shared victories in the D.XXI with LLv 24 during the same conflict, downed two SBs from 2nd SBAP on his first combat mission in BW-351.

Following the large scale aerial offensive of 25 June, Soviet activity declined over the next 72 hours. However, during the last three days of the month the Brewsters destroyed 12 aircraft in several more combats. Among the kills credited to the unit were two MBR-2 flying boats downed by 3/LLv 24's deputy leader, Pekka Kokko, on 29 June. He was

Roughly camouflaged and under armed guard, BW-352 of 2/LLv 24 rests between missions at Selänpää on 25 June 1941. The fighter was assigned to SSgt Eero Kinnunen at the time, and he used it to become an ace during the course of two missions on this very day when he claimed 4.5 SB bombers shot down. He had previously scored 3.5 victories with the D.XXI during the Winter War. The 2nd Flight colours consisted of a black propeller spinner and a black rudder, with a white tactical number applied to the latter (*SA-kuva*)

flying BW-379 over the Gulf of Finland at the time, and these victories took his overall score to five and one shared.

The Soviet bombing offensive, which ran from 25-30 June, had seen 39 attacks (totalling 992 individual sorties) against Finnish and German air bases. The Luftwaffe had suffered no losses during this period, as it had already moved its aircraft to captured Soviet airfields, whilst Finnish casualties comprised just two lightly damaged machines. In response, Finnish fighters claimed 34 bombers (out of a force of 300) shot down.

On 29 June the Finnish Air Force commander instructed LeR 2 that it was to fly top cover for the 100,000-strong Karelian Army that had been formed to retake the territory north of Lake Ladoga ceded to the USSR in the Winter War peace treaty. With Vesivehmaa deemed to be too far from the frontline, the bulk of the unit moved to Rantasalmi in early July.

The massing of Finnish troops in preparation for the offensive did not escape the attention of Soviet reconnaissance aircraft, and in early July the enemy increased its aerial activity south of Lake Ladoga. Fighter units escorted the bombers in attacks on the Karelian Army as it formed up, aircraft being drawn from the 7th Army's 55th SAD (mixed aviation division), which controlled 72nd SBAP and 155th, 179th, 197th and 415th IAP (fighter air regiments).

On 8 July LLv 24 claimed eight Soviet aircraft shot down during three combats that produced two aces. SSgt Lauri Nissinen was credited with two I-153s destroyed (in BW-353), these successes adding to his four and two shared kills from the Winter War. Nissinen's combat report stated;

'I was flying in 1Lt Kokko's swarm, leading the top pair. Above Enso, I observed two "Chaikas" and an R-5 reconnaissance biplane at an altitude of about 500 metres below me, and to my left. I attacked the R-5 from above and left, opening fire at 100 metres. The tracers hit the fuselage behind the pilot, and I noticed that the gunner did not return fire. I was then attacked by one of the "Chaikas", which twice forced me to break away from the R-5. I dived away on both occasions, and the second time I pulled up steeply and flew straight at the Russian fighter. We made several firing passes at each other from head-on until I finally hit the "Chaika's" engine, which started to pour smoke. The aircraft's landing gear also dropped down.

'I could not follow the fighter down, however, because I was forced to fend off the second "Chaika", which had slipped in behind my tail. Diving away, I then reversed direction and turned back towards the Russian fighter. We made two head-on passes and then the "Chaika" pilot tried to flee at low altitude – I quickly caught him up. The enemy pilot failed to notice me, as he continued to fly straight ahead at a height of just 20 metres above the ground. By then only my starboard fuselage gun was working, so I got in very close behind the "Chaika's" tail before I opened fire. The machine immediately burst into flames and crashed in the woods at Enso, on the western side of the river.

'I found that the "Chaika" was more manoeuvrable than the Brewster, for after four or five tight turns in opposing directions the Russian fighter was on my tail. The BW is considerably faster, however.'

The second pilot to 'make ace' on 8 July was none other than squadron commander Maj Gustaf Magnusson, who despatched a TB-3F bomber in BW-380 for his fifth kill. The following day Magnusson led a

Deputy leader of 2/LLv 24 and ranking Winter War ace, 1Lt Jorma Sarvanto leans on the tail of BW-357 at Selänpää in late June 1941 after shooting down the first of the fast Petlyakov Pe-2 bombers to fall to the Finns. The white victory bars atop the rudder refer to Sarvanto's Winter War haul (including six on 6 January 1940), while the two yellow bars at the extreme right of the lower row denote his Continuation War kills. All of these victories were over Soviet bombers. Sarvanto's final two successes would come in April and May 1943 when he downed a Yak-1 and a Yak-7 (*A Donner*)

dozen Brewsters on a patrol over Lahdenpohja, and in a short, but fierce, ten-minute battle the Russians lost eight aircraft out of a formation of fifteen fighters and bombers. Nissinen again scored a 'double', as did future ranking Finnish ace WO Ilmari Juutilainen, who claimed his third and fourth victories. The latter, in BW-364, submitted the following combat report after the mission;

'I observed 1Lt Kokko and his wingman engage the I-153 formation. I then attacked the enemy gaggle, followed by Cpl Huotari – we both fired at several aircraft from close range. Moments later I spotted an I-153 just ten metres above the ground heading for Lahdenpohja. I dived after it and opened fire from a distance of 50 metres. The fighter crashed into the forest between Miinala and Lahdenpohja.

'I then went after two aircraft that 1Lt Karhunen had initially attacked. They were heading for Sorola Island, and I held off attacking them until the trailing I-153 had formed back up with his leader. I then dived in behind the wingman and fired off half-a-dozen rounds with both fuselage guns – my wing guns did not work at all throughout the flight. The I-153 dived away to port, rolled onto its back and crashed into Lake Ladoga. My engine then began to run roughly so I broke off my chase of the lead aircraft and returned home.'

The Karelian Army offensive began on 10 July, with LLvs' 24 and 28 being ordered to secure air superiority over the advancing troops and provide fighter escort for artillery spotting aircraft. As it transpired, there was little Soviet air activity in response to the Finnish push north, except for a handful of reconnaissance missions. This in turn meant that the Brewsters patrolling to the northeast of Lake Ladoga fought relatively few engagements. The only major clash occurred on 13 July when six fighters from 2/LLv 24 that were patrolling over Tolvajärvi intercepted a mixed formation of Soviet aircraft, three of which were shot down. SSgt Eero Kinnunen, in BW-352, reported;

'At 1230-1300 hrs our flight spotted three SBs, with four I-16s flying top cover, southeast of Tolvajärvi. I attacked the latter, and a turning dogfight soon ensued. One I-16 dived away to the southeast, levelling off 100 metres above the ground. I went after it, opening fire with several bursts from directly behind the fighter. Hitting the I-16, it rolled to port and crashed into the forest.'

Ilmari Juutilainen became the next Finnish Brewster ace when he destroyed a 'Chaika' on 21 July. He was flying one of six 3/LLv 24 aircraft scrambled to intercept Soviet fighters from 65th ShAP (attack air regiment) that were strafing Finnish troops near Käkisalmi. Juutilainen claimed one of the three I-153s that were subsequently shot down.

1Lt Jorma Karhunen's 3/LLv 24 was ordered to support the offensive against the Karelian Isthmus, which was scheduled to commence on 31 July. The unit's opponents, drawn from the 23rd Army, consisted of 5th SAD's 7th and 153rd IAPs and 65th and 235th ShAPs.

Appropriately marked with a black '1' on its rudder, BW-380 was the personal mount of LLv 24 CO, Maj Gustaf Magnusson. It is seen here at Rantasalmi shortly after Magnusson, who had four kills from the Winter War, claimed a DB-3 in it to 'make ace' on 8 July 1941. The fighter exhibits 4th Flight markings, namely a white rudder with a black number and a red/white striped spinner (*SA-kuva*)

Sgt Nils Katajainen of 3/LLv 24 was the first genuine Brewster ace, claiming his fifth victory with the aircraft on 12 August 1941. Three of his first five victories came in BW-368, the tail section of which is seen in this informal shot taken at Mantsi in late September 1941. Most 3rd Flight machines featured elaborate kill tallies at this time. Katajainen would score 8.5 victories with BW-368 (*N Katajainen*)

BW-361 and BW-377 of 1/LLv 24
await their next sorties at Mikkeli in
July 1941. BW-361 was assigned to
future ace 1Lt Joel Savonen at this
time, and he claimed his first victory
in it on 16 July. 1st Flight aircraft
featured blue propeller spinners
and rudders, the latter adorned
with white numbers (*J Savonen*)

Future 10.5-victory ace 1Lt Urho
Sarjamo of 4/LLv 24 fastens his
parachute harness whilst standing
on the port wing root of BW-383 at
Rantasalmi in early August 1941.
This aircraft was actually assigned
to MSgt Martti Alho, who used it
to score all 13.5 of his Brewster kills
(*U Sarjamo*)

On 1 August 1Lt Karhunen's seven fighters destroyed six I-16s near Rautjärvi, WO Ilmari Juutilainen (in BW-353) claiming two of them;

'Between 1600-1610 hrs, in a battle against eight I-16bis that started over the frontline between Immolanjärvi and Rautjärvi, I destroyed two fighters. I set one on fire just as its pilot attempted to get in behind 1Lt Kokko, while the second one dove straight into the ground after I shot it off 1Lt Karhunen's nose. I also got onto the tail of a third one and fired at it from close range, but the fighter successfully dived away into the smoke that hung over the battlefield. I did not see it again.

'The BW is more manoeuvrable and climbs better than the I-16bis.'

The heaviest combat over the Karelian Isthmus was fought on 12 August when Capt Jorma Karhunen led six Brewsters from 3/LLv 24 on a patrol of the Antrea area. Here, they attacked a formation of about 20 aircraft from 65th ShAP. The combat, which commenced at 1300 hrs, lasted 30 minutes. During this time the Finns claimed nine 'Chaikas' shot down, with Sgt Nils Katajainen (in BW-368) getting two to make him the first 'all-Brewster' ace.

WO Ilmari Juutilainen, in BW-364, was again successful sending three down;

'1Lt Strömberg shouted over the radio "'Chaikas' below, heading north", and I quickly spotted them. I repeated his call and attacked the rearmost aeroplanes, as did Sgt Huotari. Other BW pilots also engaged the enemy a few minutes later. I counted some 22 I-153s as I dived after them. I managed to catch the fighters by surprise, and after a long burst the first camouflaged I-153 started to smoke, banked slowly to the right and went vertically down. The pilot went in with the aircraft. I attacked my second victim from above and behind, and several pieces flew off the aircraft as it continued to fly straight ahead. Moments later it fell away in a spin, and as far as I could see nobody got out of the fighter.

'Spotting another I-153, I quickly got in behind it and hit it hard with a single burst from close range – so close that oil from the Russian fighter's engine splashed all over my Brewster. My opponent, who took no evasive action, banked away to the right. Following him down to a height of about 1000 metres, I watched the I-153 crash between Kirvu and Koljola. Again, the pilot did not bail out.

'I also attacked my fourth victim from directly behind, and when he started to slowly bank away I fired another burst at the fighter, before flying over it. When I turned back to finish him off he had disappeared.

'In all, I fired at ten aeroplanes, all of which were camouflaged.'

The pilots of LLv 24 had quickly found that the 'pendulum' attack was the most effective against the slower, but more manoeuvrable, I-153 and I-16 fighters. Making full use of their height advantage, Brewster pilots would dive down and make a quick firing pass, before using their excessive speed to pull up to altitude once again.

By 21 August the Karelian Army had achieved all of its immediate objectives and started to regroup in preparation for the next offensive. LLv 24 took advantage of this lull in the action to pull all of its flights (bar 3/LLv 24) back to Immola for a brief period of rest.

On 2 September Finnish troops on the Karelian Isthmus reached the outer defensive lines surrounding Leningrad, at which point the Finnish Commander-in-Chief, Marshal Carl Gustaf Emil Mannerheim, halted the offensive in this area. The following day 'Detachment Luukkanen' was formed to cover the next advance of the Karelian Army from Tuulos to the River Svir. Its 12 Brewsters flew to Lunkula Island, on the northeast coast of Lake Ladoga, where they operated from a dry beach airstrip.

VI Army Corps of the Karelian Army waged a *Blitzkrieg* campaign from 3 September, and within 72 hours it had advanced 75 kilometres into enemy territory. The leading units reached the River Svir at Lotinanpelto at dawn on 7 September, and the following day the Germans captured the southern coast of Lake Ladoga. Leningrad came under siege.

On 12 September LeR 2 ordered LLv 24 in its entirety to the Olonets Isthmus, northeast of Lake Ladoga, where it was to protect the VII Army Corps as it advanced towards Petrozavodsk. Capt Luukkanen's 1st Flight, based at Nurmoila, was ordered to support the VI Army Corps in its crossing of the River Svir. By the 16th the three remaining flights had arrived in the Olonets Isthmus, with 2 and 3/LLv 24 being sent to Mantsi Island and the 4th Flight to Lunkula.

Pilots of 3/LLv 24 gather in front of BW-365 at Rantasalmi on 8 August 1941. They are, from left to right, Sgt Nils Katajainen, Cpl Paavo Mellin, Sgt Jouko Huotari, flight leader Capt Jorma Karhunen, deputy flight leader 1Lt Pekka Kokko, WO Ilmari Juutilainen, 1Lt Georg Strömberg and 2Lt Kim Lindberg. All but Strömberg reached ace status, and five members of the flight ultimately received the Mannerheim Cross. The latter individuals were, in order of receipt, Juutilainen, Nissinen, Karhunen, Wind and Katajainen (*SA-kuva*)

The offensive to take Petrozavodsk commenced the following morning, and Capt Per Sovelius' 4th Flight was tasked with providing fighter cover for Finnish troops. The Brewster pilots attacked 14 Soviet fighters near the target city, downing eight of them. Sovelius' pilots had identified their foes as being MiG-3s, although in actuality they had engaged LaGG-3s of 238th IAP. Deputy flight leader 1Lt Iikka Törrönen, in BW-385, became an ace during the course of this mission, the pilot describing his two victories in his combat report;

Pilots of 1/LLv 24 pose for a photograph at Rantasalmi in July 1941. They are, from left to right, WO Viktor Pyötsiä, Capt Eino Luukkanen (flight leader), SSgt Paavo Mannila and Cpl Curt Ginman. Pyötsiä was already an ace from the Winter War when this shot was taken, and although the other pilots all scored victories with the Brewster, only Luukkanen subsequently became an ace – on 6 October 1941 (*C Ginman*)

'While flying as the leader of the swarm providing top cover for our troops, I attacked five MiG fighters. I fired at one obliquely from behind, the aircraft suffering numerous hits in the fuselage before it fell away in a spin. After this I fired at another obliquely from ahead. This time I hit the fighter's engine, and it smoked heavily until it crashed. After pulling up, I observed four more MiG fighters. By now my swarm was together once again, and we immediately attacked the Russian aircraft. I fired at one obliquely from behind, saw numerous hits and watched the fighter go down in a spin. I then attempted to attack a fourth MiG, but its pilot went into a dive and I could not catch it. Running low on fuel and ammunition, I broke off the chase and returned to base.'

On 19 September Capt Karhunen of 3/LLv 24 was leading a six-aircraft patrol of the Pyhäjärvi area when he spotted three SBs from 72nd SBAP, escorted by LaGG-3s (erroneously identified as Polikarpov I-18s by the Finns) of 238th IAP. Three Soviet aircraft were shot down, with MSgt Lauri Nissinen claiming two;

'We saw three SBs dive out of the clouds and level off just above the ground. I circled beneath the clouds directly over the aircraft so that I could observe their national markings. It was at this point I noticed three I-18s to my left. This confirmed that the bombers were Russian, so I quickly targeted the rightmost SB before the I-18s could latch onto my tail. I opened fire from close range and hit the bomber's port engine, causing the SB to burst into flames and crash into the heavily wooded area below us. The remaining two bombers were also downed moments later, and we then formed up in order to take on the I-18s.

'While in the process of joining up, I spotted a single fighter coming directly towards me from below. I could not determine its nationality, so I dived away and then pulled up alongside the machine in order to identify it. I quickly realised that the aircraft was an I-18, so I throttled back and pulled in behind it. Opening fire from close range, the fighter was soon trailing both smoke and fuel from its port wing. My guns then jammed. I managed to stay behind my foe while hastily cocking the guns in an effort to free the jams. I eventually got two of my weapons to function and shot at the I-18 again from close range. The aircraft subsequently crashed into the forest.

'The aircraft were flying at a height of 50-100 metres when I attacked them in BW-384, which returned to base with six bullet holes in it.'

At 1330 hrs on 23 September, Capt Jorma Karhunen of 3/LLv 24 led seven other Brewsters in an attack on three I-16s from 155th IAP that were strafing Finnish infantry near Derevyannoye – all three Soviet fighters were shot down. The Finnish pilots then left the area for 30 minutes, maintaining total radio silence during this period, before returning to Derevyannoye again and finding six more I-16s attacking troops. Only one Soviet machine got away. 1Lt Pekka Kokko, in BW-364, recalled;

'I was leading the swarm flying top cover for our troops near Derevyannoye when three I-16s appeared in front of us. I got onto the tail of the lead aircraft and fired at it from a distance of 100 metres down to 20 metres. I saw hits behind the engine, and also holed the aircraft's auxiliary tank beneath the starboard wing. It dived straight ahead at a 35-degree angle, and my wingman, Cpl Mellin, also fired a short burst into it just before the I-16 crashed into the forest and exploded.

'Thirty minutes later I observed another three-aeroplane I-16 patrol slightly above us. By gaining altitude I got onto the tail of one of the Soviet machines, but when I attempted to open fire my guns jammed. Breaking away from the enemy aircraft, I eventually managed to get my guns operable again. By now two of the I-16s were already being engaged by other Brewster pilots, but I spotted the third attempting to flee at low altitude towards Petrozavodsk. Closing to within 50 metres of the enemy fighter, I fired several bursts at it as the I-16 skimmed over treetops at a height of just ten metres. Despite seeing numerous hits on its fuselage and wings, the fighter refused to burn. However, its engine eventually seized and the I-16 rolled over and crashed into the forest close to Petrozavodsk.'

On 26 September Soviet units suffered further losses when Capt Jorma Karhunen's formation of seven Brewsters from 3/LLv 24 downed six I-153s north of Petäjäselkä. Having already cleared the area once, the Finnish formation returned to the scene a short while later and downed three (of eight) I-15bis from 65th ShAP. Karhunen's combat report details how he claimed his fourth and fifth victories in the Brewster;

'While carrying out a reconnaissance mission over Mikonselkä railway station, I saw three I-153s flying beneath the clouds southeast of Petäjäselkä. Diving after them as they headed north at low-level, I singled out the fighter to the left of the formation. I shot him down in flames into the forest with just a few bursts of fire. After pulling up, I saw a second I-153 at low-level

A solemn looking Capt Per Sovelius, flight leader of 4/LLv 24, stands next to the tail of his Brewster (BW-378) at Lunkula in October 1941. His final score was 12.75 kills, 7.5 of which came in BW-378. The victory bars on the fighter's fin do not differentiate between shared and whole kills – Sovelius claimed four shared victories with the D.XXI in the Winter War and one with BW-378 in the Continuation War. He would eventually be appointed head of the Test Flight at Tampere (*P Sovelius*)

3/LLv 24's 1Lt Pekka Kokko taxies BW-379 in at Immola on 24 September 1941. He had already claimed 6.5 kills in this aircraft by the time this shot was taken, and he went on to score a total of ten victories with Brewsters in 1941, raising his tally to 13. Kokko then became a test pilot (*SA-kuva*)

flying in a southeasterly direction four kilometres south of where my first "Chaika" had crashed. Getting on its tail, I fired at the I-153 from a distance of 100 metres. It clipped the treetops and crashed, although on this occasion it didn't burn.

'In the second combat of this mission, at 1130 hrs, I was prevented from firing my guns at six enemy fighters – two I-15s, two I-16s and two I-153s – that I was chasing due to heavy cloud cover. During this encounter the Russian pilots took full advantage of the weather by flying in and under the clouds as they headed for the River Svir.'

The very next day eight aircraft of Capt Eino Luukkanen's 1/LLv 24 met an equal number of enemy fighters over Derevyannoye and downed three of them. Luukkanen's report stated;

'I led 1Lts Wind and Savonen, 2Lt Tervo, WO Pyötsiä and Sgts Vahvelainen, Ginman and Malin on a patrol that lasted from 1600 hrs to 1750 hrs. Four I-15s and four monoplane fighters were intercepted just beneath the clouds at Derevyannoye. The enemy pilots tried to seek refuge in the clouds, but not all of them made it. The aircraft shot up by Sgt Ginman exploded in midair, and two fighters crashed to the ground.

'Upon returning to base, our combat accounts were analysed and 1Lt Wind and I were credited with the shared destruction of an I-15, WO Pyötsiä and 2Lt Tervo shared a second I-15 and Sgt Ginman downed a third I-15 by himself.'

On 1 October the Finns captured Petrozavodsk, capital of Karelia, after which the Karelian Army continued its advance northwards along the west coast of Lake Onega. Six days later, Capt Per Sovelius' eight Brewsters from 4/LLv 24 bounced 15 Soviet fighters as they took off from Suopohja airfield, scattering them and downing five aircraft. Winter War ace Sovelius, in BW-378, claimed one destroyed and another damaged;

'I-153s and I-16s were taking of from the airfield as we approached. I attacked an I-153, and when it tried to manoeuvre out of my line of fire I slowed down behind it and hit the fighter repeatedly. It rolled over and crashed into the forest. I pulled up and went after an I-16 that I spotted flying at an altitude of 200 metres. I fired and the fighter flew through the burst, but I had to pull up to avoid colliding with it and did not see my foe crash. I fired at a second I-16, but heavy flak over Suopohja forced me to break off my attack.'

Two weeks later, on 15 October, Capt Eino Luukkanen's six Brewsters were conducting a sweep to the south of Lake Onega when they engaged

3/LLv 24 flight leader Capt Jorma Karhunen taxies out in his assigned Brewster, BW-366, at Lappeenranta in late August 1941. Although he had achieved 'acedom' during the Winter War, Karhunen initially chose not to mark the victories on the fin of his Brewster. His personal aircraft for more than two years, he would claim 17.5 kills with BW-366. Karhunen scored his final kill on 4 May 1943, in this machine, taking his tally to 31.5. By then BW-366's fin was liberally covered in white victory bars. The 3rd Flight colours consisted of an orange spinner and number, the latter applied directly onto the fighter's camouflaged rudder (*K Karhila*)

BW-382 of 1/LLv 24 sits under the cover of fir trees at Nurmoila in November 1941. Six-victory ace WO Veikko Rimminen flew this machine regularly, scoring 2.5 kills with it in August-September 1941. BW-382 enjoyed a long life in the frontline, surviving the war (*V Lakio*)

three SBs of 72nd SBAP. The latter were all ski-equipped, despite their being no snow within sight! The Finns quickly downed them, one falling to Luukkanen for his fifth victory, while WO Viktor Pyötsiä (in BW-376) claimed his fifth Brewster kill. The latter recalled;

'At 1505 hrs we intercepted three bombers over Osta. Although they turned for home as soon as they saw us, I got onto the tail of the trailing bomber as it banked to the south. I fired several bursts at the aircraft and both of its engines caught fire. The bomber went into a dive and hit the ground. Nobody bailed out. The type was unknown, on skis and with its undercarriage down. It had the speed of a DB and a fuselage like a Ju 52 when viewed from the front. Gunners returned my fire at first, and they also threw out leaflets and all sorts of other stuff.'

With winter now beginning to take a grip on the Finnish front, seven Brewsters from Capt Eino Luukkanen's 1/LLv 24 were on a search mission on 7 November to the west of the River Svir when they bounced a Pe-2 bomber escorted by three LaGG-3s of 415th IAP. Flying BW-375, Luukkanen shot down one of the fighters;

'I observed three I-18s at the same altitude (1500 metres) as us on the south side of the River Svir. I attacked with 1Lt Wind and 2Lt Suhonen, and we shot an I-18 down near Lyugovitsa – the aircraft dived vertically into the ground. The whole battle lasted just five minutes, from 0940 hrs to 0945 hrs. All three enemy fighters were shot down, but the bomber they were protecting managed to evade us due to its higher speed.

'I fired 120 rounds. The evasive manoeuvres of the enemy aircraft appeared to be very ineffective.'

By then troops of the Karelian Army had seized the Maaselkä Isthmus between Lakes Onega and Seesjärvi. They moved on to Karhumäki on 5 December, taking Povents the next day. After this the Supreme Commander, Marshal Mannerheim, ordered a halt to the advance. On all fronts the Finnish army occupied defensive positions, so starting a stalemate that lasted for the next two-and-a-half years.

WO Viktor Pyötsiä of 1/LLv 24 was assigned BW-376 at the start of the Continuation War, and the fighter is seen here at Rantasalmi in August 1941. Pyötsiä claimed 5.5 of his 8.5 Brewster kills with this aircraft. He finished the war with 21.5 victories to his name (*Finnish War Museum*)

BW-378 of 4/LLv 24 was photographed at a snowy Lunkula in December 1941. The fighter was frequently flown by Capt Per Sovelius, who used it to claim all 7.5 of his Brewster victories. BW-378 wore the inscription *Otto Wrede* on the port side of its fuselage beneath the cockpit in honour of the individual who paid for its purchase (*J Kausalainen*)

FINNISH STALEMATE

The last major combat of 1941 for LLv 24 took place on 17 December when two sections of Brewsters encountered nine Soviet Hurricanes and I-153s performing a railway reconnaissance mission over the Maaselkä isthmus. The British fighters were from 152nd IAP and the 'Chaikas' belonged to 65th ShAP. The Finns downed five aircraft, two of which fell to Capt Jorma Karhunen in BW-366;

'I led a swarm on an anti-railway reconnaissance mission. As soon as we reached our assigned patrolling area I saw three Hurricanes and six I-153s below us at a height of 1000 metres. I immediately shot down a Hurricane, followed soon after by an I-153. The Brewster pilots dominated the engagement due the employment of superior tactics. We remained above the Russians at all times, diving one at a time to attack them. The enemy formation flew at the same altitude and speed throughout, and the Hurricanes did not provide fighter cover for the I-153s.'

By year-end LLv 24 had been credited with 135 Russian aircraft destroyed in six months of combat. It had lost two Brewsters and two pilots killed in return, although only one of the losses had been in combat (1Lt Henrik Elfving in BW-385, who had been downed by flak on 3 December 1941). The 3rd Flight had accounted for 65 of the victories.

LLv 24 was operating from three locations, and this would remain the case for the next six months. The unit was now opposed by elements of 152nd IAP and 65th ShAP in the Maaselkä area, as well as 4th GPBAP (Guards bomber aviation regiment) and 415th and 524th IAPs on the Olonets Isthmus. As yet, these Soviet units still did not enjoy a numerical superiority over their Finnish foes.

At the start of 1942, LLv 24 was still led by Lt Col Gustaf Magnusson, whose HQ was at Kondupoga. The unit's 1st Flight, commanded by Capt Eino Luukkanen, flew its seven Brewsters from Nurmoila. The 2nd Flight, with Capt Leo Ahola as CO, had six fighters at Malmi, while the 3rd Flight, commanded by Capt Jorma Karhunen, flew 11 Brewsters from Kondupoga. The 4th Flight, with Capt Per Sovelius as its CO, was also based at Kondupoga with its eight machines.

As the action on 17 December revealed, by late 1941 a significant number of lend-lease Hurricanes had become operational in the Rukajärvi area to the southwest of the White Sea. These aircraft were charged with supporting Soviet troops defending

Finland's 'ace of aces', WO Ilmari Juutilainen of 3/LLv 24, claimed his first two Brewster victories in this aircraft on 9 July 1941. Twelve days later he 'made ace' in BW-353. BW-364 is seen here with its mechanic at Kontupohja (Kondupoga) in late December 1941, the fighter's fin being decorated exclusively with his Brewster claims – he scored two and one shared kills in the Winter War flying D.XXIs. The aircraft's orange number '4' can just be seen against the dark green of the rudder (*E Lyly*)

the important railway junction at Sorokka. In response, Capt Ahola's 2/LLv 24 was moved 500 kilometres northwest from Malmi to Tiiksjärvi on 8 January in an effort to counter growing enemy aerial activity over Sorokka.

The next day Capt Sovelius led four Brewsters on a patrol over the Maaselkä Isthmus, where they bounced 15 R-5 reconnaissance aircraft and their six fighter escorts near Lake Segozero. Four R-5s and a single I-153 were downed. The latter, and an R-5, were credited to 1Lt Iikka Törrönen, who thus raised his victory tally to six in the Brewster (he also had two shared kills to his name from his time flying D.XXIs).

The second all-Brewster ace was crowned on 1 February when a section of aircraft from 2/LLv 24 claimed a brace of LaGG-3s destroyed in the Käppäselkä area. The pilot in question was 1Lt Lauri Ohukainen (who later changed his surname to Pekuri), and he and ace WO Yrjö Turkka downed a single Soviet fighter apiece.

On the morning of 6 February, the 3rd and 4th Flights of LLv 24 sent eight Brewsters (led by Capt Per-Erik Sovelius) to reconnoitre the Petrovskiy-Jam region. During the course of the flight the Finnish pilots encountered seven SB bombers escorted by 12 MiG-3s. In the brief fight that ensued, two bombers and two fighters were destroyed. WO Ilmari Juutilainen claimed both of the SBs, as he recalled in his combat report;

'I noticed the bombers at 3000 metres, and radioed the boys about them. As we intercepted the Soviet aircraft, I spotted a formation of three SBs heading for a nearby railway line and dived after them. Targeting the aircraft to the left of the formation, my fire set its port wing aflame.

Pilots of 4/LLv 24 brief at Kontupohja on 17 March 1942. They are, from left to right, MSgt Sakari Ikonen, 1Lt Aulis Lumme, 2Lt Erik Teromaa, 1Lt Hans Wind, Sgt Aarne Korhonen, 1Lt Urho Sarjamo and Sgt Martti Immonen (*SA-kuva*)

BW-351 of 2/LLv 24 is seen whilst transiting through Kontupohja in early January 1942. It was one of several Brewsters fitted with retractable skis during the winter of 1941/42 when rolled runways were hard to come by. Skis were not required the following winter, however, as the Finns had made a concerted effort to have more rolled runways available (*H Lampi*)

The SB crashed next to the railway line. Just as I started after the lead bomber, I observed a MiG fighter closing in on me. In spite of the threat posed by the latter, I managed to hit the bomber in the starboard engine, which poured out smoke and oil. Moments later the aeroplane rolled over to the right and plunged into the forest close to the railway line.

'Turning my attention to the MiG, which was above me, I managed to shoot at it as we raced towards each other. My aim was good and the fighter started to trail black smoke from its engine. The MiG banked away to the east, losing altitude as it went. Five or six more fighters then chased after me, but I shook them off after a five-minute dogfight. Enjoying a height advantage, they had each taken it in turn to come after me, and I had great difficulty in getting above them. The Russian fighters were at different altitudes, which made it difficult for me to spot them all.'

Another large-scale action took place on the morning of 26 February, when seven aircraft from Capt Jorma Karhunen's 3/LLv 24 fought 15+ MiG-3s of 609th IAP over Lake Segozero. In spite of being grossly outnumbered, the Finnish pilots claimed seven victories for the loss of a solitary Brewster (BW-359, flown by Sgt Tauno Heinonen). MSgt Martti Alho, flying BW-383, became an ace during this combat, reporting;

'I dived from 1500 metres on two MiGs west of Liistepohja, I opened fired on one of them from above and behind while in a left turn, at which point the Russian threw his machine violently to the right. Following a brief dive, the fighter levelled off just above the ground and glided westward. My tracer rounds showed that I had hit the MiG's wing roots and engine, knocking the latter out – hence the fighter's powerless glide.

'With one MiG despatched, I then went after three others. When the Russians withdrew under the flak cover protecting Juka railway station, I followed a solitary MiG in a dive. Getting onto its tail, I shot at it from directly behind, at which point it levelled off close to the ground and headed for Juka railway station. I fired a second burst from a distance of 100 metres, after which the MiG pulled up, rolled to starboard and crashed into the forest next to a swamp southwest of Kärkijärvi.

'I fired 680 rounds, and flak was shot at us throughout the battle.'

In an effort to avoid losses to flak, LLv 24 rarely flew strafing missions. Occasionally, however, the unit was given approval to go after ground targets, such as on the morning of 4 March when MSgt Lauri Nissinen's section from 2/LLv 24 attacked parked aircraft near Suikujärvi. Nissinen's recounted;

'At 0715 hrs I received an order from Capt Ahola to lead four fighters (MSgt Nissinen in BW-384, 2Lt Pokela in BW-381 and Sgts Peltola in BW-352 and Lehto in BW-372) in an attack on two DB bombers and one I-16 fighter on the ground near Suikujärvi. During my first strafing pass, machine gun fire from a nearby island scored five hits on

MSgt Lauri Nissinen and his mechanics pose in front of BW-384 at Tiiksjärvi in March 1942. On 5 July 1942 Nissinen became the second squadron member to be awarded the Mannerheim Cross after claiming 20 victories (12.5 in BW-384) in the Continuation War. Although assigned to 2/LeLv 24, Nissinen's Brewster still bears the markings of the 3rd Flight, with whom the pilot had scored most of his victories prior to this photograph being taken (*Finnish War Museum*)

BW-368 of 3/LLv 24 has its engine run up at Kontupohja in February 1942. Flown primarily by SSgt Nils 'Nipa' Katajainen, the fighter's fin features six victory bars, these having been claimed by its assigned pilot between 28 June and 26 September 1941 – four of them in BW-368. The aircraft's white winter camouflage was created by the mixing of chalk powder and glue, which was then applied 'in the field' by brush (*N Katajainen*)

WO Ilmari Juutilainen was LLv 24's first Mannerheim Cross recipient on 26 April 1942, having achieved 20 victories in the Continuation War between 9 July 1941 and 28 March 1942. Proudly wearing his medal, Juutilainen is seen here posing with his assigned fighter, BW-364, at Hirvas (*R Lampelto*)

my aeroplane. I silenced the weapon on my second run, thus allowing us to target the aircraft without further interference. The Soviet machines didn't catch fire, however, although they smoked occasionally. I expended 1500 heavy and 1000 light rounds during the attack.'

The unit engaged the enemy in the air once again five days later when Capt Jorma Karhunen's eight Brewsters from 3/LLv 24 intercepted ten MiG-3s and a solitary SB east of Lake Segozero. Five aircraft were downed for the loss of BW-362, flown by ace Sgt Paavo Mellin. The latter, who was captured, had fallen victim to LaGG-3s of 609th IAP. The bomber, from 80th BAP, was shot down by Sgt Nils Katajainen (in BW-368);

'While flying over Liistepohja at a height of 400 metres I observed an SB with MiG-3 escorts. I targeted the SB, firing at it four times before it crash-landed on the ice with both engines trailing smoke. I then strafed it, leaving the bomber in flames. Within a few minutes I was dogfighting the MiG escorts. Flying head-on at one of them, I fired a long burst at my foe whose engine then trailed smoke as the MiG shot past me. I banked tightly around to get on the aircraft's tail but by the time I had completed my turn the Russian machine had vanished.'

On 27-28 March 3/LLv 24, which had been seconded to LeR 3, moved south to Immola in preparation for the Finnish Army's offensive on Suursaari, in the Gulf of Finland. From here, the flight flew top cover for ground forces as they advanced towards the Haapasaaret Islands and then on to Suursaari. During the morning of 28 March, 1Lt Osmo Kauppinen's five Brewsters of 3/LLv 24 fought ten 'Chaikas' of 11th IAP and shot five of them down. WO Ilmari Juutilainen continued his run of success when he claimed two;

'I flew as part of the top patrol with Sgt Huotari. Over the Suurkylä shoreline at Gogland we observed enemy fighters beneath us and dived down to attack them. I singled out an I-153 and shot at it several times from a distance of 50 metres until the fighter suddenly rolled onto its back at a height of 200 metres and crashed into the ice. Sgt Huotari and I then chased two I-153s to Lavansaari, where I sent a second machine down in flames – it crashed on the western shoreline of Suurkylä.

'The Russian aircraft fired rocket projectiles at our Brewsters, these weapons creating a large black, heavy flak-like, cloud when they detonated. The rockets exploded 100-200 metres ahead of my aeroplane. The I-153s carried four such rockets under both wings.'

These victories took Juutilainen's tally to 22 kills, some 20 of which had been claimed with the Brewster between 9 July 1941 and 28 March 1942. This run of outstanding successes during the Continuation War saw Juutilainen become LLv 24's first recipient of Finland's highest military decoration, the Mannerheim Cross, on 26 April 1942.

The day after Juutilainen had taken his tally to 22, 4/LLv 24 sent a patrol led by 1Lt Hans Wind to reconnoitre Segesha-Nopsa.

Simultaneously, a second patrol, led by 1Lt Iikka Törrönen, headed for Poventsa-Pelyaki. Both met a handful of R-5s, and each claimed one shot down. Wind was one of the successful pilots on this occasion, his kill making him an ace.

As the offensive progressed the number of aces continued to mount, with Sgt Heimo Lampi becoming the next to tally five kills with the Brewster on 30 March. He was flying one of eight machines led aloft by 1Lt Lauri Ohukainen of 2/LLv 24, the formation being sent to reconnoitre the Seesjärvi-Ontajärvi

Isthmus. East of Rukajärvi they bounced 12 Hurricanes of 152nd IAP that were flying in two groups. Thanks to the element of surprise, the Finnish pilots succeeded in downing eight fighters. Two were credited to Lampi (in BW-354), who wrote in his combat report;

'At 1550 hrs we spotted a formation of six-seven fighters below us at an altitude of 500 metres. Diving down to attack them from head-on, I initially fired at two aircraft but failed to see any results. I then fired at a Hurricane flying ahead and below me, and this aeroplane rolled onto its back at a height of 300 metres and crashed into the forest. Spotting a second formation of Hurricanes arriving from the southeast, I fired at two aeroplanes but missed my targets. The Hurricanes then attempted to flee, and I chased four of them with Sgt Koskela. Singling out a fighter that was just 80 metres above the ground, I hit it repeatedly until it crashed into the forest – the wreckage smoked profusely.

'We had fought with some 12 Hurricanes in total, and during the initial phase of the engagement they had held their own. However, once they attempted to disengage and head for home, they did not even bother manoeuvring in order to throw off our aim. Their sole intent was to reach their base as quickly as possible. This in turn made them easy targets.'

The next major aerial action took place on 6 April when a formation of 26 Soviet fighters and bombers targeted the Finnish air base at Tiiksjärvi, which was situated close to the enemy-held town of Segesha. The latter had been targeted by Finnish bombers the previous day, so this attack was almost certainly mounted in retaliation. The approaching aircraft were spotted by Finnish observers, and eight Brewsters from LLv 24 that were already aloft on a reconnaissance mission were diverted to intercept the enemy formation.

Pilots from 2/LeLv 24 use models of a Brewster and two Hurricanes to recreate a recent mission in front of BW-356 at Tiiksjärvi on 26 May 1942. These men are, from left to right MSgt Eero Kinnunen, 1Lt Lauri Ohukainen (later Pekuri), SSgt Heimo Lampi, Sgt Paavo Koskela, Sgt Urho Lehto, 1Lt Väinö Pokela, Sgt Osmo Lehtinen, SSgt Eino Peltola and Sgt Sulo Lehtiö. Half of them duly became aces (*SA-kuva*)

SSgt Heimo Lampi of 2/LLv 24 poses with BW-354 at Tiiksjärvi after downing two Hurricanes on 30 March 1942 to 'make ace'. Lampi subsequently enrolled in the reserve officer course and returned to his unit with the rank of second lieutenant in early 1944. Claiming HLeLv 24's last Brewster victory on 2 April 1944, he ended the war with 14 victories to his name (*H Lampi*)

Although wearing 4th Flight colours, BW-387 was actually assigned to 2/LeLv 24 when photographed at Tiiksjärvi in May 1942. Future 33-victory ace 2Lt Olavi Puro claimed four kills with it during the large-scale aerial battles of April and May 1943 (*Finnish Air Force*)

BW-390 of 1/LLv 24 was assigned to 2Lt Kai Metsola and photographed at Nurmoila in April 1942. Metsola, who scored six of his ten victories in Brewsters, claimed his first three kills in this aircraft between August and October 1941. BW-390 was destroyed in an air raid on Nurmoila on 29 May 1942 (*Finnish War Museum*)

The DB-3s of 80th BAP, escorted by Hurricanes from 609th and 767th IAPs, were engaged just before they commenced their attack. The LLv 24 pilots brought down two DB-3s and no fewer than 12 Hurricanes without loss. The leader of the Brewster unit, 1Lt Lauri Ohukainen, reported;

'At 1525 hrs, while returning from a reconnaissance mission, I received an air surveillance message that seven bombers and 18 fighters were approaching from the south. We engaged them 20 kilometres from Tiiksjärvi. I attacked the fighters while two Brewsters took on the bombers. During the course of the combat I shot my first aircraft down five kilometres southeast of the base, and it burned fiercely once it hit the ground. I struck a second machine in the engine and radiator and left it smoking heavily at a height of 800 metres south of Ontrosenvaara. Finally, I chased a fighter down to the deck and sent it crashing into the forest at Rukajärvi. The pilot was wounded and taken prisoner. I shot at six or seven aircraft in all. The Hurricanes had 12 gun wings. The Soviet pilots appeared to be generally helpless when it came to aerial combat.'

Eight days later 3 and 4/LLv 24 moved to Hirvas, which would prove to be the unit's final base in Karelia. Again, the squadron was tasked with providing fighter cover for Finnish troops from this airfield, and it also performed intercept sorties over the Maaselkä region. However, with the ice in Kondupoga harbour melting, the winter season was effectively over.

Hirvas was very much in the wilds of the Maaselkä region, and the spring thaw made the airfield all but unusable for much of April. On 31 May the 1st Flight rejoined the body of the squadron at the base, but 2/LeLv 24 (the abbreviation of *Lentolaivue* officially changed from LLv to LeLv in May 1942) remained at Tiiksjärvi. On 8 June, five Brewsters from the latter flight, led by 1Lt Lauri Ohukainen, took off from Tiiksjärvi and headed east. As they approached Kesä airfield near the Murmansk railway line, the fighters bounced three Hurricanes, which were then joined by ten more. Five Hurricanes from 152nd IAP were subsequently downed for the loss of BW-394. Its pilot, 1Lt Uolevi Alvesalo, managed to evade capture after force-landing, and soon returned to Finnish-held territory.

On a more positive note for the unit, MSgt Lauri Nissinen scored his 20th kill of the Continuation War during this action, and he was duly awarded the Mannerheim Cross a month later.

The next large-scale action involving the Brewsters took place on 25 June to the northeast of

Lake Segozero. Patrols from both the 3rd and 4th Flights struggled for 15 minutes against Hurricanes of 152nd IAP, and although 3/LeLv 24 downed four fighters and the 2nd Flight three, BW-372, flown by ace 1Lt Lauri Ohukainen, and BW-381, with Sgt Kalevi Antilla at the controls, were lost. Ohukainen recalled;

'At 1335 hrs I took off with three other Brewsters on an alert mission. West of Segesha we rendezvoused with the swarm led by WO Juutilainen. A few minutes later he attacked a formation of Hurricanes that had taken off from a nearby airfield. Sgt Anttila and I remained above the dogfight as top cover, circling at an altitude of about 5000 metres. When the battle shifted southeast I followed at a height of about 3000 metres.

'Suddenly, we were bounced by a MiG and four Hurricanes. I observed a Hurricane fire at Anttila and score hits on his engine before I could assist him. Attacking Antilla's foe at close range, the Soviet fighter fell away in a vertical dive and crashed into a swamp beneath us. By then I had four enemy fighters on my tail. I last saw Anttila gliding away to the west alone, his engine having been knocked out. I dived for the ground, and after a short dogfight I managed to lose my pursuers.

'Two more Hurricanes bounced me at a height of 4000 metres some 12 kilometres north of Lake Kalitsin. One of them scored hits on my engine, rear armour plate and port wing fuel tank, setting the later alight. Manoeuvring hard to avoid further bursts of fire, I managed to get onto the Hurricane's tail and hit it with a number of rounds from close range. It too burst into flames and disappeared to the south trailing smoke. A few minutes later my engine stopped, and whilst trying to ditch in a small lake 15 kilometres north of Lake Kalitsin, the second Hurricane hit my starboard tank. This burst into flames, setting the whole Brewster on fire.

'Flying at 250 km/h at a height of just ten metres, I pushed the nose of the fighter over and hit the lake hard, flipping the Brewster onto its back. I dived out of the inverted machine and swam ashore. The fighter sank in just 30 seconds. After walking some 20 kilometres I reached a Finnish outpost south of Lake Jolmozero. Troops here had seen one of my Hurricanes crash, starting a forest fire where it had hit the ground.

'About 15 Hurricanes and MiGs had participated in the battle. On this occasion the British-built fighters seemed to be much faster than our Brewsters at higher altitudes, as well as being quite manoeuvrable.'

BW-372 of 2/LLv 24 is seen at a cold Tiiksjärvi in March 1942. The fighter was assigned to deputy flight leader 1Lt Lauri Ohukainen at the time, and he was shot down in it by a Soviet Hurricane on 25 June 1942. Ditching the burning fighter in a small lake, he walked back to Finnish lines. This aircraft was recovered from the lake in 1998 and put on display in the Finnish Air Force Museum 11 years later (*H Lampi*)

Despite having lost an unprecedented two Brewster Model 239s on 25 June, 2/LeLv 24 had nevertheless claimed no fewer than 45 Hurricanes destroyed over the previous six months. Following the action of 25 June, the unit's sector of operations entered a quiet phase that lasted several weeks as the Soviet air forces based in the southern sectors of the Karelian Front were transferred north to protect the Allied convoys that were now arriving with increasing regularity at the ports of Murmansk and Archangel.

OVER THE GULF OF FINLAND

Despite the arrival of fine summer weather, Soviet aerial activity along Finland's eastern border had generally decreased by mid 1942. However, to the south in the Gulf of Finland region, there were ominous signs that a new Russian offensive was in the offing. The Soviets initially attempted to break the sieges of Leningrad and Kronstadt, the latter being home to a huge air and naval base. Aviation assets in this area were controlled by the air forces of the Red Banner Baltic Fleet. Included in its order of battle were a bomber aviation brigade comprised of three regiments – 1st GMTAP (Guards mine torpedo regiment), 73rd BAP and 57th ShAP (assault regiment), totalling 60 aircraft – and a fighter aviation brigade with five regiments – 3rd and 4th GIAPs and 11th, 21st and 71st IAPs, whose overall strength totalled 90 aircraft.

To counter this threat the Finnish Air Force decided to transfer its most potent fighter unit, LeLv 24, closer to the area. On 18 July the squadron duly became part of LeR 3, and on 1 August the bulk of its aircraft were flown to Römpötti, on the Karelian Isthmus. A week later the 1st Flight also arrived from Suulajärvi. Up to this point in the Continuation War the squadron had been credited with 227 victories for the loss of just eight Brewster Model 239 fighters (six in aerial combat, one to flak and one in a bombing raid).

Between 7 and 13 August LeLv 24 attempted to intercept Russian aircraft flying to the west from the Koivisto-Seiskari-Suursaari area. They enjoyed little success, however, as the enemy machines always flew well south of Seiskari Island. It thus proved impossible for the Brewsters to reach the area in time based on reports received from the Seivästö observation post. The following week new tactics were developed that allowed the Finnish fighters to be in position in advance of the Russian aircraft arriving on the scene.

The first of four large aerial battles with the enemy took place at 1030 hrs on 14 August when Capt Jorma Karhunen's six Brewsters of 3/LeLv 24 intercepted Hurricane-equipped 3rd GIAP and shot six fighters down. Two hours later 1Lt Hans Wind's five machines from 1/LeLv 24 engaged 13 Hurricanes and claimed three shot down into the sea. Wind, in BW-393, was credited two of them, as he described in his combat report;

WO Yrjö Turkka's BW-357 boasts 2/LeLv 24's 'farting elk' emblem at Tiiksjärvi in July 1942. Turkka, who became an ace on 25 June 1941, made ten Brewster victory claims. He survived the war with 17.5 kills to his name (*SA-kuva*)

SSgt Jouko Huotari helps Sgt Emil Vesa fasten his seat harness prior to flying a mission from Hirvas in BW-364 on 27 June 1942. Vesa scored 10.5 Brewster victories and Huotari 9.5. Ilmari Juutilainen had claimed two Hurricanes destroyed in BW-364 48 hours prior to this photograph being taken (*SA-kuva*)

3/LeLv 24's SSgt Jouko Huotari, Sgt Emil Vesa and WO Ilmari Juutilainen watch their fellow pilots performing aerobatics over Hirvas on 27 June 1942. All three pilots became double-figure aces. Juutilainen's BW-364 dominates the photograph (*SA-kuva*)

'While leading four other Brewsters on a dedicated interception mission we encountered 13 Hurricanes over the Tolbukhin lighthouse. I attacked two aircraft that were flying some 100 metres below the main formation, hitting the Hurricane to port with two short bursts – it fell away into the sea from a height of 500 metres. His leader then turned into me and I was forced to fire at him from head-on. We then began a turning dogfight that saw us spiralling down towards the ground. After three to four minutes I managed to get in behind the Hurricane and fire a burst at it from a distance of 20 to 30 metres. My fighter was immediately covered in oil from the Hurricane, and it fell away in a steep dive into the forest at Oranienbaum.

'With the windscreen of my fighter liberally covered in oil, I had little choice but to return to base, as I could only see ahead of me by sliding open the canopy and sticking my head out into the slipstream.

'I had fired 280 0.50-calibre and 125 0.30-calibre rounds. The Hurricane pilots, who flew with open cockpits, were wearing goggles.'

During the afternoon of 16 August Capt Jorma Karhunen's 3/LeLv 24 encountered a large enemy formation from 4th GIAP and he subsequently reported that his flight had shot down 11 I-16s. Karhunen himself claimed three aircraft, while SSgt Nils Katajainen sent down two fighters in BW-373. The latter recalled;

'I fired at one I-16 as it tried to turn away from me, and my first burst found its target. The fighter headed for the ground trailing smoke. My second victim was also hit whilst in a turn, and it crashed into the sea in a shallow dive.'

Two days later, the largest air combat of the Continuation War to date took place after LeLv 24 received reports that ten I-16s had been sighted flying eastwards over Tytärsaari at around 2000 hrs. 1Lt Hans Wind scrambled with an eight-strong formation of Brewsters and headed for

Seiskari to await the Russian fighters' return. However, they were bounced by a much larger force of Soviet aircraft upon their arrival over Seiskari. Capt Jorma Karhunen's and 1Lt Aulis Lumme's sections were immediately scrambled to assist Wind and his men, who were battling an estimated 60 Russian aircraft.

No fewer than 16 of LeLv 24's fighters were eventually embroiled in this huge dogfight, and some 16 Soviet aircraft were claimed destroyed for the loss of BW-378 and pilot 2Lt Aarno Raitio, who was killed. Triple victories were credited to Wind, Juutilainen and Karhunen (in BW-388), the latter recalling;

'After receiving word that 1Lt Wind's flight had been bounced, I scrambled with my swarm and headed for Seiskari. As we neared the area I observed 20+ I-16s flying top cover for ten patrol boats. Within moments I was on the tail of an I-16. Hitting it with several short bursts, the fighter started to trail black smoke, which developed into a raging fire. It then dived into the sea. I made a head-on firing pass at a second fighter minutes later, before going after a third machine that I spotted flying just above the sea.

'As I pulled up after attacking the latter fighter, five more I-16s came after me from above. I fired at one from head-on, hit it directly in the engine. The fighter flick-rolled onto its back and crashed into the sea. The remaining four I-16s chased me away to the northeast, where I spotted a solitary Pe-2 bomber flying just above the waves. Having shaken off the Soviet fighters, I was free to attack the lone twin-engined bomber, which I shot down in flames into the sea.

'The 60+ I-16s were split up into several separate formations, staggered in altitude. The Soviet pilots seemed more than prepared for a fight on this occasion. Upon my return to base I discovered that a single machine gun round had struck my starboard aileron.'

Karhunen had now taken his Continuation War tally to 20, in addition to the five and three shared victories he had claimed during the Winter War. The ace was awarded the Mannerheim Cross two weeks later.

Despite being grossly outnumbered during these actions over the Gulf of Finland, the Brewster pilots had a major advantage over their Soviet counterparts. LeLv 24 had seen plenty of action in other sectors over the previous 18 months, thus allowing its pilots to hone their flying skills and combat tactics. The unit's appearance over the Gulf of Finland also took the Red Banner Baltic Fleet completely by surprise. Indeed, the Brewster Model 239 was not even mentioned in Soviet recognition manuals in this sector of the frontline! LeLv 24 took full advantage of all these elements to claim no fewer than 39 Soviet aircraft destroyed in just one week, and 50 during the whole of August. These losses had rocked the Red Banner Baltic Fleet to the extent that there was very little Soviet air activity over the Gulf of Finland for the rest of the month.

On 20 September Capt Jorma Karhunen was leading six Brewsters from 3/LeLv 24 on a patrol of the Kronstadt-Tolbukhin-Seiskari area when, nearing the Estonian coast, they were bounced by ten fighters. The veteran pilots soon turned the tables on their attackers, however, downing three Soviet fighters. WO Ilmari Juutilainen claimed two in BW-364;

'I followed Capt Karhunen into the attack after we were set upon by ten MiGs and Spitfires. In the ensuing combat I managed to shoot at a Spitfire in a turn, sending it down trailing smoke in an inverted dive into the sea four kilometres southeast of Peninsaari. I then targeted a MiG from below and behind, sending it crashing into the sea in flames. I also fired at a second MiG but without success.

'The Spitfires were fast, had a good rate of climb and were highly manoeuvrable. My engine did not run properly throughout the dogfight.'

A little over a month later, on 22 October, Capt Eino Luukkanen and his wingman from 1/LeLv 24 intercepted an Il-4 of 1st GMTAP

3/LeLv 24 flight leader Capt Jorma Karhunen, test pilot Capt Pekka Kokko and Karhunen's pet dog 'Peggy Brown' pose in front of BW-366 at Römpötti when the latter ace paid a visit to his old unit on 29 September 1942. Karhunen shot down eight aircraft in just three combats in mid-August 1942 and was awarded the Mannerheim Cross on 8 September 1942. Some 17.5 of his 25.5 Brewster victories were claimed in BW-366 (*SA-kuva*)

(misidentified as a Pe-2) and several I-16s whilst patrolling over Seiskari-Retusaari. Luukkanen, who already had 13 victories to his name, achieved his first double victory in the subsequent dogfight;

'At 0930 hrs we spotted a Pe-2 at a height of 400 metres. As I made a firing pass at the bomber, I saw four fighters about 20 kilometres away to the southeast. Breaking off our attack, we went after the fighters

instead. These aircraft turned out to be I-16s, and I shot at one from behind as it flew below an overcast of cloud at a height of 500 metres. The fighter caught fire and dived into the sea. I attacked a second I-16 head-on, with visible results. My third opponent was also engaged from head-on, and I saw it crash into the forest, cutting through a swathe of trees.

'Having used up all of my ammunition, I broke off the fight and flew at a height of just ten metres above the ground to Kreivinlahti. Here, I observed another four I-16s 200 metres above me. Anxious not to be detected, I remained at treetop height and managed to avoid combat.

'I had used 700 0.30-calibre and 660 0.50-calibre rounds, of which half had been fired at the Pe-2 – I also saw the latter drop a torpedo.'

Three days later 1/LeLv 24 sent three Brewsters, led by 1Lt Joel Savonen, to patrol the Lavansaari-Seiskari area. The Finnish pilots intercepted four Hurricanes of 3rd GIAP escorting two Pe-2s. News of their find prompted 3/LeLv 24 to despatch Capt Jorma Karhunen and four Brewsters to the area, and in the subsequent dogfight all of the Soviet fighters were shot down. Future ace 1Lt Väinö Suhonen (in BW-376) claimed two of the Hurricanes, as he described in his combat report;

'At 1400 hrs, while flying at a height of 500 metres, our three-aeroplane patrol engaged a formation of fighters and bombers in the Tolbukhin-Kronstadt area. I fired a short burst at a Hurricane from above and behind and it crashed into the sea. I then fired at a second fighter from side-on and a third from above and behind – the latter fell away in a dive. I was dodging bullets from a fourth Hurricane at the time, which meant that I couldn't see whether the third machine crashed or not.'

Shortly before noon on 26 October, six Brewsters of Capt Karhunen's 3/LeLv 24 surprised two DB-3 bombers and their escorts over the Oranienbaum coast. Five of the Finnish machines went after the escorts, downing two of them, while ace MSgt Eero Kinnunen (in BW-351) claimed both of the bombers destroyed. Thirty minutes later, 1Lt Hans Wind and his flight of five Brewsters from 1/LeLv 24 engaged 15 fighters in the same area, shooting four of them down into the Gulf of Finland. Wind (in BW-377) wrote in his combat report;

'I spotted four I-16s north of Kreivinlahti heading towards Seiskari. We attacked them, and the aerial battle quickly moved in the direction of the Shepelevskiy lighthouse. A few minutes into the dogfight at least 11 more I-16s arrived on the scene.

'I briefly followed an I-16 through a series of tight banking turns before shooting it down in flames from a height of about 20 metres. The aircraft

BW-355 of 3/LeLv 24 sits idle between sorties at Römpötti in October 1942. This aircraft was assigned to SSgt Leo Ahokas, who claimed seven Brewster victories in an overall score of 12. He downed two LaGG-3s with this aircraft on 23 September 1943. The purchase of this particular fighter was funded by well known Finnish company Nokia Oy, and it and bore the inscription *NOKA* on the forward fuselage (*O Puro*)

Nine-victory ace 1Lt Joel Savonen of LeLv 24 was a member of the 1st Flight throughout the Continuation War, and he later became one of the few reservists to be assigned leadership of a flight. All bar one of Savonen's kills were claimed with the Brewster (*V Lakio*)

2/LeLv 24's MSgt Eero Kinnunen sits atop the leading edge of BW-352's horizontal tailplane at Tiiksjärvi sometime after he claimed a Hurricane kill in this machine on 8 June 1942. Kinnunen was subsequently shot down and killed in this aeroplane on 21 April 1943, having by then increased his score to 22.5 victories. He was the highest scoring ace to perish at the controls of a Brewster (*A Donner*)

crashed into the forest on the western shore of Lake Harjavallanjärvi. I then went after eight I-16s that were below me, hitting one of them in the central fuselage area with a long burst of fire. The aeroplane rolled onto its back at an altitude of 50 metres and ploughed through trees as it crashed into the forest about half-a-kilometre southeast of Shepelevskiy lighthouse. I fired at three more I-16s but to little avail.

'The I-16s we encountered preferred to fight us on the deck, where the Russian fighter proved to be far more manoeuvrable than the Brewster.

'An incendiary bullet hit the wingtip of my machine, which caused the wing to smoke heavily for about 30 seconds until the fire had burnt itself out. My fighter's port stabiliser was also holed during a frontal attack.'

More I-16s were engaged on 30 October, again over Oranienbaum, when Capt Eino Luukkanen's detachment from 1/LeLv 24 intercepted eight machines from 4th GIAP as they escorted a solitary Pe-2. Three I-16s and a single Brewster (BW-376) were destroyed in a dogfight that lasted 20 minutes. This action proved to be high-scoring ace Luukkanen's last mission in the Brewster, and once again he was flying BW-393;

'I observed eight I-16s at a height of 1000 metres. My wingman and I were leading a second pair of Brewsters that were some 400 metres above us, and the latter swarm immediately attempted to attack the I-16s. However, neither formation could gain a height advantage over the I-16s, so we had to break off our pursuit and concentrate on attaining more altitude. As we climbed to 3500 metres, so the I-16s tried to match us – they eventually reached 3400 metres astern of us.

'By then the Soviet machines were above Lake Harjavallanjärvi, and my swarm attacked the aircraft from the south out of the sun as they were flying in a large defensive circle. The latter had a width of about a kilometre, and it was some 100 metres below us.

'During the engagement I fired at three I-16s, one of which went down in a vertical dive trailing smoke from its fuselage. I was then set upon by other fighters, which forced me to dive near-vertically down to a height of about 1000 metres. When I pulled out I saw two Spitfires and a Pe-2 below me. I attacked one of the Spitfires from the rear and it crashed into the forest and exploded.

'Sgt Paavo Tolonen did not return from this mission, and his disappearance was not observed by anyone.

'In addition to the eight I-16s that we had initially attacked, there were four more below them. I saw four Polikarpov fighters crash into the forest, including the I-16 that I had shot down.'

BASE MOVE

LeR 3 transferred the 1st, 3rd and 4th Flights of LeLv 24 to the captured airfield at Suulajärvi, on the Karelian Isthmus, on 15 November. The base had been refurbished by the Russians between the wars, and it was captured by Finnish troops virtually intact.

On 21 November five aircraft from the 2nd Flight took off from Tiiksjärvi and flew to Immola. The following week they too headed to Suulajärvi, where the whole squadron found itself together as a single unit for the first time since the start of the Continuation War. Its area of operations remained the western Karelian Isthmus and eastern Gulf of Finland, although LeLv 24 saw very little action for the rest of the year.

Indeed, only two aerial engagements were fought in November, with the unit spending the rest of its time flying reconnaissance missions or acting as bomber escorts.

The first clash with Soviet aircraft took place on the morning of 22 November when 1Lt Aulis Lumme led five Brewsters of 4/LeLv 24 into a dogfight with six Yak-1s (identified as 'Tomahawks' by the Finns) near Kronstadt. Three enemy fighters were destroyed, as was a lone Il-2 that got caught up in the action. 1Lt Erik Teromaa claimed two victims;

'I fired at the Il-2 from above and behind until it began to smoke heavily. Its engine must have then quit, as the pilot made a forced landing. At the same time a Tomahawk latched onto my tail and shot several holes into my aeroplane. I eventually lost my attacker by pulling up into the solid overcast that blanketed the area. Coming back out of the clouds, I spotted another Tomahawk directly below me, which I fired at while turning in behind it. The aircraft dropped its wing and dived vertically into the sea.

'Following this engagement I can confirm that the Tomahawk is faster and more agile than the Brewster. Unlike the other Russian types I have met in the past, these machines stuck around and tried to fight us. Indeed, the Tomahawk pilot who bounced me remained glued to my tail despite my best efforts to shake him.'

After re-arming and refuelling, 1Lt Lumme's detachment returned to the same area several hours later and, together with Capt Jorma Karhunen's six Brewsters from 3/LeLv 24, downed an Il-4 bomber and three fighters. Both Lumme and Teromaa 'made ace' during the course of the day.

On 23 November LeLv 24 fought three separate aerial battles almost simultaneously in the Lavansaari-Kronstadt-Kreivinlahti area. The first involved the 4th Flight, with 1Lt Aulis Lumme's five Brewsters being pitted against four Pe-2s and their six escorts. Two of the bombers, a Tomahawk and a Spitfire (probably a Yak-1) were downed by the Finns.

A short while later 1Lt Hans Wind of the 1st Flight led his section against a similar formation. He and his wingman destroyed two Pe-2s and an I-16 between them, Wind recalling in his combat report;

'I got in behind an I-16 and shot it down, the fighter crashing heavily on the shoreline – both of its wings were broken off and the fuselage came to rest upside down. Having witnessed the fighter's demise, I then went after three Pe-2s and a Yer-2. I shot one of the Pe-2s down into the sea, the aircraft quickly sinking. I fired four bursts into a second Pe-2, which fell away in a shallow glide towards Kronstadt. My fighter was then targeted by fierce flak, and this prevented me from confirming whether this aircraft did indeed crash. I fired at the Yer-2's fuselage from a distance of about 300 metres without effect. The Yer-2 was as fast as the Pe-2, despite it appearing to be larger. Its wings were markedly bent.'

1/LeLv 24 flight leader Capt Eino Luukkanen is seen in his flying gear at Römpötti on 1 November 1942. His Brewster, BW-393, has had its fin adorned with *Lahden Erikois* beer bottle labels in place of victory symbols. A week later Luukkanen was promoted to major and given command of LeLv 30 (*E Luukkanen*)

1Lt Erik Teromaa of 4/LeLv 24 commences his take-off run in BW-367 at Suulajärvi in November 1942, the airfield blanketed in the first snow of the winter. Teromaa scored four of his 13 Brewster kills in BW-367 (*H Malmberg*)

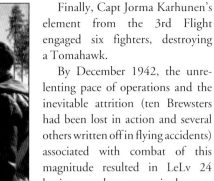

Some of LeLv 24's senior pilots discuss the recent series of fierce combats that they had fought with Soviet aircraft over the Gulf of Finland in mid-April 1943. They are, from left to right, 3/LeLv 24 leader Capt Jorma Karhunen, LeLv 24 commander Lt Col Gustaf Magnusson, 2Lt E Riihikallio, 2/LeLv 24 leader Capt Iikka Törrönen, Sgt Kosti Keskinummi, 2Lt Jorma Saarinen and MSgt Martti Alho (*SA-kuva*)

MSgt Eero Kinnunen's BW-352 is seen here during a visit to Hirvas on 7 August 1942. It fell to a La-5 of 4th GIAP on 21 April 1943 over the Gulf of Finland, but not before Kinnunen had downed a LaGG-3 and a Yak-1 – the latter was a shared kill (*E Rinne*)

Finally, Capt Jorma Karhunen's element from the 3rd Flight engaged six fighters, destroying a Tomahawk.

By December 1942, the unrelenting pace of operations and the inevitable attrition (ten Brewsters had been lost in action and several others written off in flying accidents) associated with combat of this magnitude resulted in LeLv 24 having to be reorganised as a three-flight unit so as to keep each of the flights equipped with eight fighters. Thus on 11 February 1943, its order of battle at Suulajärvi saw the unit still headed by Lt Col Gustaf Magnusson, with the 1st Flight led by Capt Jorma Sarvanto, the 2nd Flight led by 1Lt Iikka Törrönen and the 3rd Flight led by Capt Jorma Karhunen.

After three months of little action, LeLv 24 participated in its first major aerial engagement of 1943 on 23 February. Flying south of Lavansaari, six Brewsters of the 3rd Flight (led by Capt Jorma Karhunen) attacked four Pe-2s and their 12 I-16 escorts from 4th GIAP. The Soviet fighters prevented the Finns from reaching the bombers, but lost six I-16s in doing so. Two fell to WO Eero Kinnunen in BW-352;

'I was part of Capt Karhunen's flight, and we were leading the top cover patrol. Intercepting a formation of Soviet fighters and bombers as it headed west over Peninsaari, I attacked an I-16 from above and behind. Breaking off my gunnery pass after I saw it trailing smoke, the fighter was then targeted by Sgt Kauppinen. Looking for more enemy machines, I spotted three I-16s heading towards me from Peninsaari. Getting in behind them, I initially attacked the fighter to the right of the formation again from above and behind. The I-16 caught fire and crashed through the ice, its pilot bailing out and luckily landing on the ice rather than in the freezing water.

'I then made three diving attacks on the fighter to the left, which fell away trailing thick smoke until it hit the open sea. In the meantime, the lead aircraft had climbed up to my altitude, forcing me to make head-on firing passes at it. After several tight turns, the I-16 managed to get onto my tail and open fire, at which point I broke away in a steep dive and headed for home.

'The I-16s were dispersed across a wide area during the battle.'

LeLv 24 next saw action on 10 March when eight fighters from the 2nd Flight intercepted seven Pe-2s, escorted by ten LaGG-3s from 3rd GIAP (misidentified as MiG-3s by the Finns), as they approached Kotka. The formation was engaged in the Haapasaari area, 1Lt Iikka

Its winter camouflage heavily weathered, BW-386 of 2/LeLv 24 awaits a well-earned overhaul at Immola in March 1943. Previously assigned to 6.5-victory ace MSgt Sakari Ikonen (who claimed three victories with it), the fighter was passed on to 1Lt Urho Sarjamo when the former became an instructor. Sarjamo claimed six victories with BW-386 between 18 April and 12 December 1943. Note the 2nd Flight's osprey emblem on the fighter's fin (*E Laiho*)

Törrönen leading the attack. When the Soviet aircraft abandoned their mission and turned for home, the Finns chased them across the Gulf of Finland to Oranienbaum. One of the bombers and six LaGG-3s were downed during the pursuit, which was eventually ended by a fierce flak barrage around Oranienbaum. 2Lt Eero Riihikallio described the melee in his combat report;

'I saw a MiG-3 attacking one of our Brewsters. When the latter outmanoeuvred the MiG-3, the Soviet fighter pulled up directly in front of me. I fired several bursts at it from close range and it fell away to starboard and crashed on the ice about two kilometres northwest of Seiskari. I subsequently fired at two more MiG-3s before being forced to break off my attacks by heavy flak.'

April saw a significant change over the Gulf of Finland when Soviet aerial activity increased and there was a major improvement in both the equipment the enemy fielded and the tactics they employed. In addition, the newly-built airfield at Seiskari became operational and the runway at Lavansaari was extended so that Pe-2s and the new generation of more capable Soviet fighters could operate from there. The fighter escort provided for the Il-2s and Pe-2s was now more sophisticated in terms of the tactics used, and this in turn meant that LeLv 24 rarely had the opportunity to attack them. The bombers were given direct cover, usually by manoeuvrable I-153, Yak-1 or LaGG-3 aircraft staggered at different altitudes, with wider tactical cover provided by newer La-5, Yak-1 and Yak-7 fighters in separate formations up to an altitude of 6000 m. Finally, fighters from Krasnaya Gorka and Kronstadt also flew up to Seivästö to keep the Brewsters engaged well away from the bombers.

DANGEROUS ENEMY

On 14 April LeLv 24 participated in the first in a series of fierce aerial battles involving the unit when 1Lt Hans Wind led four 1st Flight Brewsters over the eastern Gulf of Finland to engage 30 LaGG-3 (misidentified as Spitfires) and La-5 fighters as they escorted bombers flying in from the west. Five Soviet fighters were shot down into the sea, two of them falling to 1Lt Kim Lindberg to give him ace status;

'We spotted enemy aeroplanes directly below us and I attacked the closest one to me – an La-5. Diving down to a height of 200 metres, I got in behind the fighter and opened fire from a distance of 70 metres. Hitting the La-5 hard, it fell away in a vertical dive and crashed into the sea. I then targeted a Spitfire that was flying at an altitude of 150 metres. The fighter, which was heading north, began trailing white smoke from its engine after my very first burst of fire. This attack took place 12 kilometres south of Seiskari. I was prevented from confirming the Spitfire's fate by two of his squadronmates, who chased me out of the area.'

Four days later another large-scale aerial clash took place over the Gulf of Finland. 1Lt Aulis Lumme of 2/LeLv 24 had led six Brewsters aloft at

1/LeLv 24 aces WO Viktor Pyötsiä and 1Lt Kai Metsola share a joke at Suulajärvi after their successful combat with the Soviet Baltic Fleet air forces on 18 April 1943. The unit had claimed 19 aircraft shot down that day, of which Pyötsiä claimed two and Metsola one (*V Lakio*)

1700 hrs, followed five minutes later by seven more machines from the 1st Flight, led by 1Lt Joel Savonen. The fighters had been scrambled to intercept eight Il-2s from 7th GShAP, and their 50-strong fighter escort from 3rd and 4th GIAPs, near Kronstadt. The subsequent battle lasted for an hour, during which time the Finns shot down two of the *Shturmoviks* and no fewer than 18 fighters without loss. It was a stunning victory for LeLv 24.

Lumme (in BW-370) claimed both an Il-2 and a LaGG-3, as noted in his combat report;

'Having scrambled, we encountered eight Il-2s and at least 25 fighter escorts (eight La-5s, nine LaGG-3s and eight Yak-1s) east of Seiskari. Fierce combat continued uninterrupted for 45 minutes as the enemy formation headed towards Kronstadt. The Il-2s dropped down to an altitude of just five metres, and the escorting fighters stuck to their assigned task by remaining with them.

'I fired at an Il-2 from above, behind and from the side, all at very close range. The aeroplane banked to the left, hit the sea and sank. Minutes later, after a short turning fight, I managed to shoot at a LaGG-3 from behind at very close range. The fighter began trailing smoke and then banked over into the sea. I also fired at another 20+ fighters during the course of the engagement, some of which I definitely hit.

'Our flight's tally of 11 aircraft shot down wouldn't have been so high had the fighter escorts not been forced to remain at slower speeds in order to stick with the Il-2s. Indeed, both the LaGG-3 and the Yak-1 are considerably faster than our slow Brewsters.'

All three of LeLv 24's flights were in action on 21 April, when the unit intercepted 35 LaGG-3, Yak-1 and La-5 fighters of the Baltic Fleet air forces as they escorted Il-2s between Seiskari and Kronstadt. Capts Joppe Karhunen and Iikka Törrönen each led six aircraft aloft at 0800 hrs to intercept the enemy formation, and shortly after the battle commenced, Capt Jorma Sarvanto came to his squadronmates' assistance with five more Brewsters. They could not prevent La-5s of 4th GIAP shooting down SSgt Tauno Heinonen (in BW-354) and 22.5-victory ace WO Eero Kinnunen (in BW-352) – both men were killed. In return, the Finns claimed 19 victories.

Törrönen, who downed both a LaGG-3 and a La-5, described his kills in his combat report;

'Given the order to scramble, I took off with my flight of six Brewsters and headed for the Gulf of Finland. Nearing Peninsaari, I observed five Il-2s and their escort of six LaGG-3 and Yak-1 fighters. Once the latter had spotted us, they went into a dive. By the time we caught up with them to the east of Seiskari they were already down on the deck. The Soviet machines had flown straight into a trap, as Capt Karhunen and his flight were laying in wait for them. A fierce dogfight with the escorts then took place, and more enemy aircraft joined in until there were 20 to 30 Soviet fighters in the immediate area.

'I fired at several enemy machines before focusing my attacks on a LaGG-3 that had begun to trail smoke – it eventually crashed into the forest near Lipeva village. My wingman, 2Lt Riihikallio, and I were then set upon by three La-5s over Tolbukhin-Kronstadt. I managed to get onto the tail of one of the fighters just as it settled into a firing position

behind 2Lt Riihikallio. Hitting the La-5 hard, the fighter began belching out smoke and crashed on the northwest shoreline of Kronstadt Island.

'The enemy fighters had once again stuck to their escort duty.

'This action confirmed that the new La-5 was highly agile and completely superior to the Brewster both in terms of its maximum speed and rate-of-climb.'

On 2 May the Red Banner Baltic Fleet air forces sent a handful of Il-2s, escorted by 20+ fighters, to attack Finnish troops emplacements in the town of Kotka. They were engaged by 18 Brewsters to the south of the target, resulting in an hour-long battle being waged across the Gulf of Finland. 2/LeLv 24 destroyed four LaGG-3s, but had 11.25-victory ace, and flight leader, Capt Iikka Törrönen (in BW-380) shot down and killed in return – he fell victim to a LaGG-3 from 10th GIAP.

The two Soviet fighters credited to 2Lt Olavi Puro during this clash gave him ace status. He described their demise in his combat report;

'We intercepted an enemy formation between Someri and Haapasaari as it headed southeast. I attacked the LaGG-3s that were escorting Il-2s in the direction of Lavansaari. Getting in behind one of the fighters, I opened fire at a distance of between 50-100 metres. Firing regular bursts, I chased my victim for three kilometres, descending all the time. Finally, at an altitude of 150 metres, one of my bursts hit the cockpit and the LaGG-3 dived into the sea about ten kilometres southwest of Someri.

'1Lt Sarjamo and I then chased three enemy fighters east of Lavansaari, at which point we were bounced out of the sun by eight more LaGG-3s. After a series of tight banking turns, I managed to fire a burst at one of my attackers that hit it between the engine and canopy. Panelling flew off the fighter and flames poured back towards the cockpit. Burning profusely, the LaGG-3 crashed halfway between Lavansaari and Peninsaari.

Photographed in the blast pen at Hirvas in June 1942, BW-380 was assigned to 4/LeLv 24 flight leader 1Lt Iikka Törrönen. He went on to claim 11 victories, all bar one in Brewsters, prior to being killed in action in this machine fighting LaGG-3s of 10th GIAP over Oranienbaum on 2 May 1943 (*Finnish War Museum*)

Formerly WO Ilmari Juutilainen's mount, BW-364 of 3/LeLv 24 was photographed here at Immola in late April 1943. All of Juutilainen's 36 aerial victories are marked on the fighter's fin, 28 of them having been scored in this particular aircraft. Juutilainen was second only to Hans Wind in the number of Brewster victories that he claimed (*E Laiho*)

'I fired at at least another six enemy fighters, one of which hastily landed at Lavansaari airfield. Low on ammunition, the Russian machines finally broke off and headed east.

'During the dogfight I found that the Brewster could pull tighter turns than the LaGG-3, and that our speeds were comparable when on the deck. The Russian pilots that we encountered were both aggressive and enterprising.'

Forty-eight hours after this engagement, 12 Brewsters attacked five Il-2s and their ten I-153 close escorts. Top cover for the Soviet formation was provided by 12 LaGG-3s. Intercepting the enemy aircraft near Seiskari, the Finns downed nine Russian machines. Sgt Jouko Lilja perished, however, when his fighter (BW-388) was shot down by a LaGG-3 from 3rd GIAP. 1Lt Hans Wind (in BW-393) claimed no fewer than four kills during the clash;

'Flying as wingman to Capt Karhunen, I spotted four I-153s and five Il-2s over Peninsaari. Diving down onto the tail of one of the "Chaikas" as it raced along at low-level, I opened fire and the biplane rolled over onto its starboard wing and plunged into the sea.

'Despite our appearance, the Il-2s continued heading for their target in Kopornoye Bay. I managed to slip in behind them whilst the other Brewster pilots kept their fighter escorts busy. Approaching one of the *Shturmoviks* from the port side, I hit it in the wing root. The aeroplane instantly caught fire and crashed into the sea. I then shot down a second Il-2. I got my third *Shturmovik* as the formation neared Shepelevskiy, the aircraft beginning to smoke prior to it hitting the sea off Tolbukhin. Throughout this engagement, the only evasive manoeuvre attempted by the Il-2s was to side-slide. The ground attack aircraft caught fire very easily when hit in the wing root.'

Finnish fortifications at Suursaari were bombed by the Russians on 9 May, and during the day LeLv 24 recorded its 500th victory. The first encounter saw 15 Brewsters tangling with the bombers' 30+ escorts, two of which were downed by 1Lt Hans Wind's 3rd Flight. In the second encounter, five 1st Flight aircraft (led by Capt Jorma Sarvanto) and four 2nd Flight machines (led by 1Lt Aulis Lumme) claimed a Yak-7, although it was misidentified as a Tomahawk. 'Spitfires' were also reported, although they were almost certainly Soviet-built types such as the LaGG-3 or Yak-1/7.

Three more aerial battles were fought by LeLv 24 around Seiskari on the morning of 20 May. The 2nd Flight was initially scrambled, and

BW-393 was assigned to 1/LeLv 24's 1Lt Hans Wind after he was promoted to fill the vacancy left by former 1st Flight leader Capt Eino Luukkanen in November 1942. He had already claimed six kills with the fighter prior to it being passed on to him by the departing Luukkanen, and Wind would score a further 20.5 victories with BW-393 through to late September 1943. Seen here on patrol over the Karelian Isthmus in late April 1943, Wind's most successful mission in the fighter came a few days later on 4 May when he claimed an I-153 and three Il-2s, thus taking his tally at the time to 25 kills (*J Sarvanto*)

A landing gear malfunction forced the pilot of BW-370 to ditch in Lake Immolanjärvi on 1 May 1943. Having been designed for service with the US Navy, the aircraft stayed afloat and was eventually towed to shore. BW-370 was assigned to 2/LeLv 24 deputy leader 1Lt Aulis Lumme at the time of the accident, and he claimed 4.5 of his 11.5 Brewster victories in it. He ended the war with a tally of 16.5 kills (*K Bremer*)

its pilots claimed two LaGG-3s destroyed. A short while later the 1st Flight downed a Yak and, finally, the 3rd Flight was credited with the destruction of two more Yak fighters from a formation of 30 aircraft. Several hours later LeLv 24 returned to the same area in strength, and its 14 aircraft intercepted 40+ Soviet aircraft flying in mixed formations. Seven Lavochkins and a Yakovlev fell to the Finnish guns. One of the La-5s was credited to SSgt Emil Vesa, thus giving him ace status.

During a six-week period from mid-April through to the end of May, pilots flying decidedly obsolescent Brewster Model 239s had claimed no fewer than 81 enemy aircraft shot down for the loss of just three of their own. These stunning results had been achieved through the employment of sound tactics that made the most of the Brewster's strengths – service ceiling, speed in the dive and manoeuvrability. By staggering its flights at higher altitudes and taking full advantage of the by now well-honed pendulum interception tactic, LeLv 24 had been able to inflict serious losses on stunned Russian fighter regiments equipped the very latest crop of Lavochkin and Yakovlev fighters. No longer engaging slower Hurricanes, I-16s or I-153 biplanes, the La-5 and Yak-1/7 were considerably faster than the Brewster, but this did not phase the pilots of LeLv 24.

On 30 May LeLv 24's veteran CO Lt Col Magnusson was promoted to command LeR 3, and his place was taken by Capt Karhunen. 1Lt Wind was in turn made leader of the 3rd Flight.

Six days later, on the afternoon of 5 June, all three flights (numbering 16 aircraft) intercepted two Russian formations comprised of four Pe-2s, seven to eight Il-2s and 10-15 fighters. The Brewsters shot down a Pe-2, an Il-2, an La-5 and three Yakovlevs without loss. Sgt Onni Avikainen claimed a Yak-1 and a Pe-2 to attain ace status;

'I spotted ten fighters and four Pe-2s south of Tolbukhin and attacked the formation. I closed on a Yak-1 from above and behind, firing a single burst at it before pulling up in preparation for a second attack. However, as I commenced climbing I saw that the aeroplane I had fired at had ditched into the sea. Observing four Pe-2 north of Tolbukhin, I attacked the bomber furthest to the right in the formation from above and behind, and kept firing until I was within 30 metres of my target. Breaking off my attack and diving away to the right of the bomber, the latter exploded seconds after I had flown past it.'

Following more than seven weeks of frenetic activity, when the Soviets had thrown formation after formation at the Finnish fighter force, the rest of June and all of July was mercifully quiet for LeLv 24. Additional Soviet fighter units had been moved into the newly built air base at Seiskari, and they protected bombers and ground attack aircraft returning from missions to the German front. Many interception patrols were flown by the Brewster pilots during this period, but it proved increasingly difficult for LeLv 24 to engage Russian formations. The latter now remained close to the south coast of the Gulf of Finland, the bombers at sea level and the escort fighters staggered at several altitudes above them.

Things got worse for the unit when Soviet aircraft began flying patrols between Oranienbaum and Seivästö, as the Il-2s and Pe-2s were all but out of range of the Brewster pilots. Also, in order to avoid unnecessary losses to the now depleted Model 239 force, LeLv 24 was forbidden from flying over areas known to be well defended by flak.

1Lt Väinö Suhonen of 1/LeLv 24 and SSgt Tapio Järvi of 2/LeLv 24 are seen at Suulajärvi in May 1943. Suhonen finished the war with 19.5 victories and Järvi 25.5. The former claimed 4.5 Brewster kills and the latter 9.5 (*V Lakio*)

Mannerheim Cross winner 1Lt Hans Wind of 3/LeLv 24 poses with BW-393 in September 1943. The fighter's fin sports 33 victory markings, to which Wind later added six more. Claiming 39 victories with the Brewster, Wind was the top scoring Model 239 pilot (*SA-kuva*)

3/LeLv 24 leader 1Lt Hans Wind taxies BW-393 in at Suulajärvi on 12 September 1943. Having claimed 39 kills with the Brewster, he went on to score a further 36 in the Bf 109G between 27 April and 28 June 1944. HLeLv 24's top ace, Wind was twice awarded the Mannerheim Cross (*SA-kuva*)

With the arrival of Bf 109G-equipped LeLv 34 in the frontline, LeLv 24 was posted an area east of the Viipuri-Oranienbaum line so as to give the obsolete Brewsters a better chance of engaging the enemy on more equal terms.

On 31 July 3/LeLv 24's commander, 1Lt Hans Wind, was awarded the Mannerheim Cross after taking his tally to 33 victories (all scored in Brewsters).

Having seen little action for more than two months, 16 Brewsters (and three Bf 109Gs) fought a large-scale combat over the Gulf of Finland on 20 August. The Finnish pilots engaged a similar number of LaGG-3s and La-5s south of Seivästö, LeLv 24 shooting down six Soviet fighters and heavily damaging a seventh. Three LaGG-3s fell to SSgt Emil Vesa and his patrol, as the ace recalled in his combat report;

'I was flying top cover for the flight led by 1Lt Wind, and had Sgt Kauppinen as my wingman. I dived on two LaGG-3s and scored many hits on one of them, as did Sgt Kauppinen. The aeroplane started to trail smoke as it banked round Tolbukhin and headed for Kronstadt, and after crash-landing it burst into flames. I immediately pulled up and went after two more LaGG-3s in a turning dogfight. I hit one of them as it dived for the ground and saw it crash on the beach at Yhinmäki – the wreckage smoked profusely. I then fought with several other fighters but saw no visible result for my efforts.'

Eleven days later 1Lt Urho Sarjamo of 2/LeLv 24 led his six Brewsters against a formation of Il-2s and their fighter escorts, shooting down one of the *Shturmoviks*. At the same time 1Lt Hans Wind's section met a pair of La-5s over Oranienbaum and shot them both down. Finally, the new leader of 1/LeLv 24, 1Lt Lauri Nissinen, attacked four Yak-7Bs of 13th KIAP with his formation of five Brewsters. Two were shot down, but Sgt Sulo Lehtiö (in BW-356) was killed in return. Nissinen wrote;

'I was the lead aeroplane in a formation of five Brewsters. As we flew south of Koivisto in a westerly direction at a height of 2000 metres, we saw four LaGG-3s below us to our right. We dived after them, and I shot

BW-357 was assigned to 6.5-victory ace SSgt Viljo Kauppinen of 3/HLeLv 24 at Suulajärvi in April 1944. *Lentolaivue* 24's abbreviated designation had changed for a third, and final, time on 14 February 1944 (*J Kausalainen*)

at one in turning fight. The fighter soon started trailing smoke as it attempted to dive away. The smoke then stopped and the LaGG pulled out of its dive, at which point I fired again. This time the fighter crashed into the sea, leaving a large slick of oil to mark where it had sunk.

'As I was finishing the LaGG off, a second Soviet fighter latched onto my tail, but I quickly turned the tables after a few tight turns. Opening fire, the LaGG also started to smoke. The pilot tried to dive away, opening up a gap of some 300 metres, but once he levelled out I slowly began to gain on him. I fired a series of bursts as the LaGG approached an enemy-held island. I was then forced to break off my attack, leaving the fighter heavily smoking – I could only see the LaGG's wingtips when directly astern of it. Moments later the Seivästö observation post "Seppo" contacted me over the radio to tell me that my LaGG had crashed near Oranienbaum.'

The last great aerial battle of 1943 involving the Brewster took place on 23 September overhead the cold waters of the eastern Gulf of Finland. Soon after 1300 hrs, four fighters from of 3/LeLv 24, led by 1Lt Martti Salovaara, and two Bf 109G patrols from 1/LeLv 34 tangled with 20 Soviet fighters close to the Shepelevskiy lighthouse. The Finns subsequently reported downing three Yakovlevs and five Lavochkins. Two-and-a-half hours later, 1Lt Hans Wind and his seven-strong formation of Brewsters attacked 15 Soviet aircraft returning to Seiskari. The Finns claimed an Il-2 and six Lavochkins destroyed. In his short combat report, 1Lt Hans Wind stated;

'I was leading the flight when we met eight Lavochkins and six Il-2s. First, I shot at an Il-2, which tried to reach Seiskari airfield after I had inflicted heavy damage on it. The *Shturmovik* crashed and burned at the south end of the runway, however. I then shot down an La-5, which ditched into the sea and sank almost immediately.'

Martti Salovaara claimed a kill on each mission to become the last Brewster pilot to reach ace status.

The skies over the eastern Gulf of Finland then became relatively quiet, with only the occasional clash between small formations of fighters until 2 April 1944, when the last Brewster kill claimed by the redesignated *Hävittäjälentolaivue* 24 was recorded – a LaGG-3 credited to ace 2Lt Heimo Lampi in BW-382. The following month all remaining Model 239s were handed over to HLeLv 26, allowing HLeLv 24 to re-equip with the considerably more modern Bf 109G.

Hävittäjälentolaivue 24, equipped with Brewsters from the beginning of the Continuation War, had claimed 459 Soviet aircraft shot down between 25 June 1941 and 21 May 1944. In the same period it had lost just 15 Brewsters in combat, four in accidents and two in air raids. Twelve of its pilots had been killed and two captured. It was an outstanding record for a much-maligned fighter.

MALAYAN CAMPAIGN

I n an effort to bolster the air defences for the Royal Navy's base in Singapore, a number of fighter squadrons were established in the Far East in early 1941. These units were primarily manned by Australian and New Zealand pilots fresh from flying training. Quite rightly deemed unsuitable for use in Europe, the Buffalo was seen as the perfect equipment for these squadrons in an area which, although tense, was at peace. There were clearly other theatres (North Africa and the eastern Mediterranean, not to mention the Channel front) that had a higher priority than the Far East for more modern British fighter types such as the Hurricane and Spitfire.

The first of these new squadrons – Nos 67 and 243 – formed at Kallang, on Singapore Island, in mid March 1941. No 67 was temporarily commanded by Flt Lt Colin Pinckney, who had gained three victories and three probables flying Spitfires with No 603 Sqn, pending the arrival of Sqn Ldr R A Milward, who took over in late July. The squadron's Buffaloes were shipped in crates directly from the USA, and the first was ready for air testing by 29 April.

No 243 Sqn was under the command of Sqn Ldr Gerald Bell, who told the author;

'We were equipped with Brewster Buffaloes, an American aircraft designed for use on carriers that had been discarded by the US Navy as obsolete. However, we were proud to be flying the Buffalo, which was, despite its obsolescence, modern when compared to the other aircraft with which RAF Far East Command was equipped.'

A number of other experienced pilots also arrived in Singapore during the course of 1941, including eight-victory Battle of Britain ace Flt Lt Tim

Newly assembled Buffaloes of No 243 Sqn, with one from No 67 Sqn beyond, sit lined up at Kallang airport in April 1941. The nearest aircraft is W8142/WP-N, which was regularly flown over the next few months by future ace Flg Off 'Blondie' Holder. Next to it is W8139/WP-B in which Battle of Britain ace Flt Lt Tim Vigors lost his propeller after a mid-air collision but managed to land safely (*P M Bingham-Wallis*)

Vigors who had been at Eton with Flt Lt Pinckney. Another pilot who joined the unit was 27-year-old Flt Lt Mowbray Garden, who was later to become the financial director of the producers of this volume, Osprey Publishing.

Among the pilots who tested the aircraft after their re-assembly were two newly qualified New Zealanders, Sgts Vic Bargh and Geoff Fisken, and they would subsequently gain a number of successes with the Buffalo. The fighter made an immediate

When No 453 Sqn RAAF arrived in Singapore, command of the unit was given to Sqn Ldr W J Harper. He is seen here in his aircraft, AN213/TD-Z, which is thought to have been the only Buffalo to have carried a personal score in the Far East – in this instance recording all of Harper's combat claims, including three destroyed (via C F Shores)

impression on them, Bargh enthusing 'I thought they were terrific – they were beautiful aeroplanes. Well, we all thought they were good, you know. We didn't know that they were out of date!'

Training proceeded apace as aircraft became available, and in June the squadrons flew their first war patrols, No 243 also sending a detachment from 'B' Flight, led by Flg Off 'Blondie' Holder, to northern Malaya. With more Buffaloes in-theatre by the summer, the first of the Commonwealth units, No 453 Sqn RAAF, arrived in late August and was placed under the command of experienced RAF pilot Sqn Ldr W J Harper. As events would prove, he was a singularly unfortunate choice. His flight commanders were Flt Lts R D Vanderfield and B A Grace, both of who had served in the UK, but all the other pilots arrived directly from training.

The Buffalo was not quite the cutting edge fighter many of these tyro aviators had hoped for. Nonetheless, training of newly arrived pilots continued, initially on the Wirraways of No 21 Sqn RAAF at Seletar. However, in September, this squadron also began converting to the Buffalo, its training task being assumed by the Operational Training Unit at Kluang, in Malaya. By the end of the month No 21 Sqn had 11 fighters on strength. On 10 October Sqn Ldr Allshorn became the unit's CO just as No 67 Sqn began moving to Burma, being replaced at Kallang by the newly formed No 488 Sqn RNZAF.

The latter unit was led by New Zealanders in the RAF, with the CO being 12-victory ace Sqn Ldr Wilf Clouston and Flt Lts John Mackenzie (ten victories) and John Hutcheson serving as the flight commanders. The new unit commenced an intensive training programme, although progress was somewhat hampered by the poor state of the Buffaloes bequeathed to it by No 67 Sqn. No 488 Sqn also suffered from a general lack of tools, spare parts and other equipment.

No 488 Sqn RNZAF was initially commanded by Sqn Ldr Wilf Clouston, a New Zealander in the RAF who had ten victories to his name following service in Britain (M Goodman)

BLOODING IN THE NORTH

With the likelihood of war with Japan looming, in mid November No 21 Sqn was ordered to move to Sungei Patani, close to Malaya's border with Thailand (then known as Siam), to support III Indian Corps. On 2 December the battleships HMS *Prince of Wales* and *Repulse* arrived in Singapore as a visible and powerful deterrent to the Japanese, and taking passage with them was Battle of Britain ace Sqn Ldr Frank Howell, who assumed command of No 243 Sqn upon his arrival in the Far East.

Flg Off Maurice 'Blondie' Holder was one of No 243 Sqn's original pilots. During the brief Malayan campaign he became one of just four pilots to achieve five victories with the Buffalo. He also flew the type's first combat sortie when he strafed landing barges early on 8 December 1941 (via B Cull)

The Japanese invasion force approached the northeast coast of Malaya on the night of 7/8 December 1941, and in the early hours the first troops came ashore after a brief bombardment. Their target was the airfield at Kota Bharu, where No 243 Sqn had a small detachment. Locally based Hudsons were the first Allied aircraft to attack the enemy, then at 0630 hrs No 243 Sqn's Flg Off 'Blondie' Holder (in AN196/WP-W) and Plt Off R S Shields (in W8221/WP-X) took off and strafed landing barges on the Kelantan River. Holder's fighter was hit by ground fire, however, and had to return to base. The Buffalo suffered further damage when it hit an abandoned Hudson shortly after landing.

Holder was at the controls of AN196/WP-W when he flew the first Buffalo sortie against the Japanese. Having been hit by ground fire, he was forced to abandon the fighter at Kota Bharu, where, as can be seen, the Buffalo fell into enemy hands (F G Swanborough)

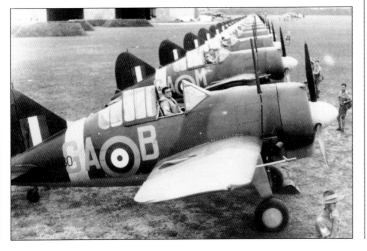

AN180/GA-B heads this line-up of No 21 Sqn aircraft photographed on 19 November 1941. AN180 saw considerable action with No 453 Sqn's Sgt V A Collyer at the controls on 22 December, the Australian pilot probably destroying a Ki-43. On 17 January Sgt Alf Clare, also of No 453 Sqn, used it to shoot down a Ki-27 and share in the destruction of a Ki-43 near Muar. These successes meant that Clare was the first Allied pilot to achieve five victories, and thus become an ace, on the Buffalo (RAAF)

No 21 Sqn RAAF received Buffaloes in place of its Wirraways just prior to the Japanese invasion of Malaya. The unit bore the brunt of the initial assault, being virtually destroyed at Sungei Patani. No 21 Sqn's W8227/GA-E was almost certainly abandoned there (*No 21 Sqn RAAF*)

Left to continue the mission alone, Shields became the first RAF Buffalo pilot to engage the Japanese Army Air Force (JAAF) when, at 0700 hrs, he spotted a formation of Ki-21 'Sally' heavy bombers. He immediately attacked them, but after a brief burst of fire his guns jammed – an experience that was to become all too familiar for Buffalo pilots over subsequent weeks.

With the coming of daylight, the enemy had sufficient forces ashore to capture the main prize of Kota Bharu airfield. It was not an auspicious start to the war in Malaya for the Allies.

Further south, shortly before dawn, Singapore suffered its first bombing raid, and in spite of having three aircraft on standby No 453 Sqn was not given permission to scramble them!

At about the same time as Holder and Shields were giving the Buffalo its baptism of fire, at Sungei Patani, on the opposite side of the Malayan peninsula, No 21 Sqn was warned of an inbound raid. Soon afterwards five Ki-21 'Sally' bombers appeared overhead the base. Although two pilots were strapped into their Buffaloes, they were initially told to await further instructions – even as the first bombs fell! They managed to get off, but on closing with the enemy they too suffered gun failures. Back at Sungei Patani, considerable damage had been inflicted by the enemy bombers. Elsewhere, other airfields in northern Malaya were attacked throughout the morning. The damage at Sungei Patani did not prevent No 21 Sqn from despatching two Buffaloes on a reconnaissance mission to Singora, in Thailand, where they were intercepted by Ki-27 'Nate' fighters of the 11th Sentai. Both aircraft managed to escape, however.

Mid-morning, with five Buffaloes on standby, Sqn Ldr Allshorn again requested permission to scramble against another incoming raid, but this was refused despite bombs raining down. With the fuel dump and further aircraft hit, the airfield was devastated, leaving just four Buffaloes undamaged. No 21 Sqn was then ordered to withdraw to Butterworth, which had also been heavily bombed. With Japanese troops on the perimeter of Kota Bharu, No 243 Sqn's detachment was also ordered to withdraw.

Buffalo W8157/TD-M was flown by Flt Lt Tim Vigors over the sinking *Prince of Wales* and *Repulse* on 10 December 1941. On 15 January 1942, whilst assigned to No 21/453 Sqn, Flt Lt Jack Kininmont probably destroyed a Ki-48 with it. Four days later he used it to shoot down a Ki-51 and a Ki-43 (*via M Goodman*)

For the RAF, it had been a quite dreadful first day, and worse was soon to follow. That evening the *Prince of Wales* and *Repulse* belatedly put to sea with an escort provided by four destroyers. This small but powerful fleet was designated 'Force Z', and it headed northwards at full speed to intercept Japanese troop transports reported off Singora, where Adm Sir Tom Phillips expected to be by dawn on the 10th.

On the morning of 9 December No 21 Sqn could muster just four serviceable aircraft. That afternoon the unit had its first combat with enemy fighters when a section of Buffaloes was bounced by JAAF fighters. One RAF machine was quickly shot down and the pilot of the second aircraft was forced to crash-land. A short while later a second pair of Buffaloes from the unit was engaged by Ki-27s, and Flg Off 'Monty' Montefiore claimed a 'Nate' shot down – the Buffalo's first victory with the RAF. Montefiore was in turn forced to take to his parachute minutes later. His companion was also badly hit and force landed. It had been a bloody first encounter with the nimble enemy fighters, and the RAF pilots had again been hampered by gun stoppages.

With Butterworth in ruins, that evening units were ordered to evacuate all surviving aircraft south to Ipoh. Worse news soon followed, as shortly after 1100 hrs the following morning 'Force Z' was attacked by Japanese torpedo-bombers. Observing strict radio, the capital ships did not report their predicament to Singapore until just before midday, by which time both vessels had been badly hit. On receipt of the signal two Buffaloes from No 243 Sqn were immediately scrambled, followed by ten more from No 453 Sqn, led by Flt Lt Tim Vigors.

First on the scene were Flt Lt Mowbray Garden and Sgt Geoff Fiskin of No 243 Sqn, the latter remembering, 'As our aeroplanes reached the rendezvous point, I could see below me a grey metal bow sticking out of the sea, surrounded by an oil slick and many bodies'. Shortly afterwards Flt Lt Tim Vigors arrived over the sinking battleships and saw hundreds of survivors in the water, recalling, 'As I flew round, every man waved and put his thumb up as I flew over him. After an hour, lack of petrol forced me to leave'.

The first confirmed victory by a future ace was made by Flt Lt Doug Vanderfield in AN185/TD-V on 13 December 1941 when he shot down three Japanese bombers near Butterworth – even though his undercarriage was stuck down throughout the engagement. Parked alongside the fighter in this impressive line-up photograph is AN210/TD-J, which Vanderfield used to claim two fighters probably destroyed on 22 December. He flew AN210 for the last time on 19 January 1942 during a Wirraway escort to Muar (*RAAF*)

RETREAT IN DISORDER

The destruction of the RAF in northern Malaya had forced it to reform those shattered units in the south, but the mood of impending doom and general malaise greatly aided the Japanese, who targeted Penang on 11 December. Some of the fighter escorts then landed at the newly captured Kota Bharu, further weakening the RAF's position. These raids were repeated the next day, and that morning four Buffaloes of No 243 Sqn, led by Flg Off 'Blondie' Holder, with Sgts Geoff Fisken, Bert Wipiti and John Oliver, were flown up to Ipoh to operate alongside the battered remnants of No 21 Sqn. Three of these pilots would subsequently become aces.

Their arrival was timely, for Penang would soon be the focus of a sustained bombing campaign as the enemy pounded the troops of the 11th Indian Division. On the 13th No 453 Sqn was also ordered to Ipoh. At 0600 hrs that same day the unit sent three aircraft, led by Flt Lt Vanderfield, to reinforce Butterworth. However, no sooner had they landed here than they were ordered off to intercept another raid on Penang harbour by Ki-48 'Lily' twin-engined bombers of the JAAF's 75th and 90th Sentais (misidentified as 'Mitsubishis' by the pilots) and three Ki-51 'Sonia' ground attack aircraft (reported as 'Stukas') of the 59th Sentai. The Buffaloes headed for cloud cover, before diving on the intruders. Flt Lt Doug Vanderfield later recalled his first step to 'acedom';

'We immediately took off and intercepted three Japanese bombers. As we attacked them, five or six dive-bombers came out of the clouds and attacked us. We let them have the works, and definitely shot down two in the first attack. A sergeant pilot in my flight fired on a dive-bomber that was trying to sit on my tail, and it rolled over and disappeared. Another went out to sea in a long dive.'

Short of fuel, the Buffalo pilots then had to land almost immediately, although Vanderfield headed directly back to Ipoh, where he was credited with two Ki-48s and one Ki-51 destroyed. These were the first victories attributed to a future RAF Buffalo ace, and Vanderfield had achieved this feat with his undercarriage stuck down! His wingmen, Sgts Read and Collyer, also claimed three Ki-51s between them.

No 453 Sqn's next Ipoh-bound formation was led by Tim Vigors, followed by Flt Lt Grace and his section. He, Vigors and three other pilots then flew on to Butterworth, but as they landed another JAAF fighter sweep appeared, so they immediately took off. Vigors soon engaged some Ki-27s but was hit in the fuel tank, as he recalled;

'We attacked these from above, giving us the advantage of surprise, and I told my wingman, Sgt O'Mara, that I was going into the middle of the enemy formation in order to break them up. The usual melee ensued, during which time I was pretty certain that I got hits on several of the Japs, but things were far too hot to bother about the score. The Army 97 could turn right inside the Buffalo, and I was a little too long in realising the extent of their manoeuvrability! As a result, I received a direct hit in the petrol tank, which was situated under my feet. Somewhat naturally, the tank proceeded to blow up in my face.'

Badly burnt on the legs, hands and arms and wounded in the thigh, Vigors bailed out, but was fired on several times by the Japanese during his descent.

All of Flt Lt Doug Vanderfield's five victories were made when flying the Buffalo. He was evacuated to Australia when Singapore fell, and later returned to operations flying Spitfires over New Guinea with No 79 Sqn RAAF (*G Scrimgeour*)

Grace's fighter had also suffered combat damage, but he managed to shoot down one of the nimble Ki-27s prior to landing back at Ipoh. Sgt R R Oelrich was shot down and killed, however, and the remaining two Buffalo pilots crash-landed. Penang was evacuated a short while later. Worse followed for No 453 Sqn later that day, as when its final Ipoh-bound formation headed north it ran into bad weather. Three Buffaloes crashed, killing two pilots.

Also in action that morning was Sgt Geoff Fisken from the No 243 Sqn detachment;

'My first encounter with the enemy took place over Ipoh aerodrome. I reckon a total of 13 Jap bombers were shot down here. "Ack-Ack" must have been responsible for some, but not all, of the damage inflicted on the low-flying bombers. It was a case of flying in and out as quickly as possible. I made my first kill (credited as a "probable" – author), a Jap Army 97 bomber, after diving on it from above.'

Despite the heavy losses suffered by No 453 Sqn on the 13th, it was No 243 Sqn's detachment that returned to Singapore the next day. The remnants of the Australian unit saw further combat with JAAF aircraft on the 14th too, Sgt Greg Board, desperately evading enemy fighters at low level, managing to get onto the tail of a Ki-51, which he hit;

'Flame mushroomed from the wings and almost at once a huge ball of red fire swept around the "Zero" (sic), the blazing mass trailing greasy smoke into the jungle, where it disappeared in a blinding explosion.'

With Japanese attacks in north and central Malaya intensifying, the lack of a warning system to alert fighter units of imminent raids forced the Buffalo squadrons to fly standing patrols. During one such mission, three Ki-43 'Oscars' swept in over Ipoh and the patrol dived down on them. The Japanese fighters easily outfought the Buffaloes, although future ace Sgt Alf Clare of No 453 Sqn was credited with his first victory.

Ipoh too was soon deemed untenable, at which point the Australians withdrew in some haste and disarray to Kuala Lumpur, from where they were again in action. In the mid-morning of the 22nd, Flt Lt Vanderfield led a dozen Buffaloes aloft. Passing through 7000 ft, the Australians sighted a large Japanese formation that included 'Me 109s'. The latter were Ki-43 'Oscars' of the 64th Sentai, led by Maj Tateo Kato. The JAAF fighter unit soon became embroiled in its first action of World War 2, which No 453 Sqn's diarist described as 'the Buffalo's last stand in Malaya'.

Bounced in the climb, the Buffalo pilots fought for their survival in a desperate dogfight that lasted ten minutes. Four pilots were posted missing, including Sgt Mac Read, who collided with a Ki-43 (possibly flown by Lt Takeo Takayama) and was killed. Sgt Harry Griffiths was credited with two Ki-27s destroyed while Vanderfield probably destroyed two more. Later in the mission Sgt Greg Board shared in the destruction of a Ki-48 'Lily' before being forced to bail out. Alf Clare was also successful, claiming three victories. These were the Buffalo's last claims over Malaya of 1941. The battle had seen the virtual demise of No 453 Sqn, and the surviving aircraft were ordered back to Singapore, where, on Christmas Day, it was amalgamated with No 21 Sqn under the command of Sqn Ldr Harper – an insensitive move, as he had little empathy with the Australians.

One of No 488 Sqn's flight commanders was Flt Lt John Mackenzie, a ten-victory Spitfire ace from the Battle of Britain. The grandson of a former Prime Minister of New Zealand, he was unable to add to his score in the Buffalo (*RNZAF*)

No 243 Sqn's first victory was a Ki-46 'Dinah' shot down on 10 January 1942. It was shared by Sgts Charlie Kronk (right) and Bert Wipiti (left), for whom it was a first step to ace status. Between them examining the wreckage is their CO, Sqn Ldr Frank Howell, who was already a ten-victory ace, and who claimed his only Buffalo kill shortly after this photograph was taken (*via C F Shores*)

—SINGAPORE *BLITZ*—

Meanwhile, back in Singapore, No 488 Sqn had continued to make progress towards attaining operational status, while on 13 December a dozen Dutch Brewsters of 2-VlG 2, under the command of Kapt Jacob van Helsdingen, had flown up to Kallang under a pre-arranged agreement. Other than the occasional scramble in an attempt to intercept the near daily Japanese reconnaissance flights, Singapore enjoyed a hiatus from attack throughout December.

In an effort to improve the island's nocturnal defences, Sqn Ldr Frank Howell had some specific night flying modifications made to two of his Buffaloes, which were also painted black. However, these aircraft had little impact on a night raid on New Year's Eve. Mowbray Garden flew one of the fighters at night, subsequently recalling, 'I never saw the enemy bombers, except for a fleeting flash of aircraft below me – only feet below me – and then nothing but the black night once again. Later, I was told that I must have flown straight through the formation of bombers, on a diagonal course, without knowing it!'

The enemy continued this nocturnal activity into the New Year, and on the night of the 2nd both Howell and Garden were up, but they were unable to make contact. The following day No 488 Sqn, followed by Nos 21/453 and 243 Sqns, provided cover for the first convoy bringing in reinforcements to Singapore – low cloud and rainstorms helped hide the vessels from the enemy, but also made the fighter escorts' mission far more challenging. Poor weather also played a part in the spate of crashes experienced by all three squadrons during the first week of January, some seven Buffaloes being written off

In an effort to better coordinate the fighter defences of Singapore, No 224 (Fighter) Group was formed, with Wg Cdr George Darley in charge of fighter operations. Battle of Britain ace Sqn Ldr Richard Brooker was also on the staff at the AHQ, and he occasionally flew with No 488 Sqn to pass on his considerable experience.

On 10 January No 243 Sqn finally claimed its first confirmed victory when Sgts Bert Wipiti and Charlie Kronk brought down a Ki-46 'Dinah' reconnaissance aircraft of the 81st Independent Chutai. It was first sighted by Wipiti, who dived onto the aircraft's tail and fired a long burst that struck one of its engines. Forced to reduce speed, the 'Dinah' was then attacked by both pilots, who chased it down, firing all the way, until it crashed into the jungle. New Zealander Kronk recalled the first of his six Buffalo claims in a newspaper interview at the time;

'I came up from underneath it and saw the big body of the aeroplane, with its great red circles on the wings right over my head. Then I pressed the tit and emptied everything I had into her. I kept firing until all my ammunition was gone. She was burning all the way to the ground, but the

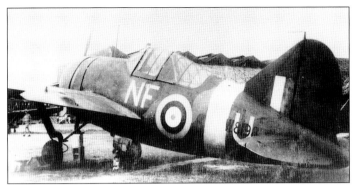

Among the aircraft assigned to Flt Lt John Mackenzie was W8198/NF-U, which was delivered to No 488 Sqn on 8 October 1941 and flown by the Kiwi ace for the first time on the 25th of that same month. The fighter occasionally appeared in his logbook through to the invasion of Malaya in December 1941, and MacKenzie sortied in it at least three times on 20 and 21 January 1942. It appears that Sgt Jim MacIntosh was the only pilot to enjoy success with the fighter, however, claiming two A6M Zero-sens probably destroyed on 18 January (*RNZAF*)

Although crudely defaced by the wartime censor, the identity of this Buffalo is W8139/WP-B of No 243 Sqn. Flt Lt Mowbray Garden was flying this aircraft in murky conditions on 12 January when he shot down a pair of Ki-27s and probably destroyed another. Three days later Sgt Rex Weber used W8139 to share in the destruction of an A6M, the latter aircraft also being attacked by Garden (*author's collection*)

Japs seemed to think that they could land her. But just as she flattened out she seemed to burst into flames all over and an enormous sheet of flame shot up and she disappeared into the treetops.'

In the same interview Wipiti was more succinct. 'I slipped down from above and gave him a burst in his motor'. No 243 Sqn pilots was delighted to steam a march on their rivals in No 488 Sqn, for whom Sgt Eddie Kuhn had almost broken their duck later that same day when he intercepted a C5M 'Babs' reconnaissance aircraft but it escaped in cloud.

Two days later the Japanese *blitz* on Singapore finally began, with elements of the JAAF moving into recently captured airfields in Malaya. Early that morning, 72 Ki-27s flew a fighter sweep over the island. In response, Flt Lt Mackenzie led off eight Buffaloes from No 488 Sqn's 'A' Flight, followed by six from 'B' Flight and three Dutch machines. 'A' Flight was soon bounced as it climbed, leaving the pilots fighting for their lives. In the squadron's first combat two Buffaloes were lost and five damaged, with no claims made by the inexperienced Kiwis in return.

Close behind the Japanese fighter sweep was a formation of 30 bombers, escorted by Ki-43s. No 243 Sqn was belatedly ordered to scramble, as was the combined Australian unit, but they both failed to make contact with the enemy. Later in the morning Mackenzie led a further patrol, as did Sqn Ldr Clouston at midday. It was No 243 Sqn that saw action, however, in the early afternoon when the Ki-27s returned once again. Flt Lt Mowbray Garden attacked one group head-on in the misty conditions and was credited with a pair of 'Nates' destroyed and a third as a probable. One of his foes came so close that its aerial dented the wing of his aircraft;

'There were three of them in formation on my tail, and I could not out-turn them. Meanwhile, they were hammering my mainplanes and fuselage with their machine guns. I was dying for an excuse to bail out until I remembered the advice of Flt Lt Tim Vigors, which was to the effect that when you think all is lost and death and destruction are imminent, just shut your eyes, work the rudder left and right, open the throttle and "pudding basin" the control column. I did just that.'

Garden managed to land his Buffalo, but it was badly shot up .

Two more Ki-27s were shot down by future ace Flg Off 'Blondie' Holder, while Sgt Geoff Fisken also claimed his first confirmed victory when he too shot down a 'Nate', commenting 'one turned towards

Seen at Kallang in early 1942, this Brewster 339D B-3110 was assigned to 2-VlG-V of the Netherlands East Indies Army Air Corps. On 12 January Lt August Deibel scrambled in it and intercepted a formation of Ki-27 'Nates', two of which were shot down before the Dutchman was wounded and forced to bail out of the fighter. Deibel, posing in front of the aircraft, claimed three victories in total (*via B Cull*)

me and I went down, and we both kept firing at one another. I recall seeing his cannon shells coming at me. Luckily, I pulled up and he went downwards. He blew up beneath me'. The explosion rendered Fisken's Buffalo temporarily uncontrollable.

No 488 Sqn was unable to make contact with the enemy, but the Dutch engaged nine Ki-27s at 13,000 ft. Lt August Diebel, at the controls of B-3110, claimed two 'Nates' shot down before being wounded and having to bail out himself. His CO, Kapt Jacob van Helsdingen, and Sgt Gerardus Bruggink each claimed a Ki-27, although the latter force landed.

On 13 January the next large Allied convoy arrived in Singapore, bringing with it a batch of Hurricanes. Heavy air attacks were anticipated, and although Imperial Japanese Naval Air Force (IJNAF) bombers set out from Borneo to attack the vessels, poor weather prevented most of them from reaching their targets. In the late morning Flt Lt J H Hutcheson led an intercept of 30 IJNAF G3M 'Nell' bombers. Attacking from astern, the Buffaloes suffered heavily from return fire, and five were written off and a sixth damaged for no enemy loss. The attack had been disrupted nevertheless, allowing the ships to dock safely.

Later in the day a formation of light bombers, with an escort of Ki-43s, was engaged by No 243 Sqn, led by Sqn Ldr Howell. Scrambling in heavy rain and thick cloud, he wrote 'We took off to engage a very large number of bombers and fighters. The Flight separated after being attacked by escorting fighters'. The Buffaloes flew into cloud for cover, and when Mowbray Garden came out again, 'Dead ahead I saw some single-engined Japanese aircraft that had not seen me. I stalked them, and when I got close enough I chose one particular victim. At that very moment he saw me and we went into a tight turn, but I was able to hold him. With a long burst I crippled him, and he dived into the ground'.

Another fighter fell to the guns of Plt Off Noel Sharp, who was detached from No 488 Sqn – his usual mount, W8138/NF-O, carried a striking green dragon personal marking. This was Sharp's second claim in successive days, having bagged a 'probable' on the 12th.

BUFFALO ACES

Bad weather again frustrated the enemy attacks on the 14th, although a section of fighters was scrambled after an IJNAF reconnaissance aircraft, and its escorting A6M Zero-sens, appeared over Singapore. Fisken was successful again when he claimed one of the escorting fighters as a 'probable', and this was later confirmed destroyed. Having modified the harmonisation of his guns and the ammunition that they fired, Fisken noted in his logbook, 'One Navy Type 0 probable – definitely damaged. Confirmed later. Eighteen bullets in own aircraft'.

This reconnaissance mission presaged a further raid that materialised early on the 15th when 27 IJNAF G4M 'Betty' bombers attacked Tengah. One of their escorting A6Ms was downed by Mowbray Garden and Sgt Rex Weber, their victim almost certainly being PO1c Hiroshi Suyama of the 22nd Air Flotilla who was lost that morning. However, Sgt J B Oliver of No 243 Sqn was killed in action. A handful of Dutch Buffaloes were also scrambled, three of them, flown by Kapt van Helsdingen, Ens F Swarts and Sgt G M Bruggink, being bounced by a number of Zero-sens. Swarts was shot down and killed during the engagement.

Later that same day the JAAF attacked Singapore City, and No 488 Sqn finally broke its combat 'duck' when Sgt Eddie Kuhn brought down a Ki-27 – the first of his four or five victories (his final score remains uncertain). Kuhn recalled;

'I came out of a layer of cloud and saw two enemy aircraft, one of which I attacked head-on. It went down into cloud, and although I never saw it crash, it landed alongside an Army base and was duly confirmed.'

Kuhn was then set upon by another fighter, which quickly damaged his aircraft. Unable to fend off his attacker, Kuhn was saved through the timely intervention of his fellow Kiwi, Noel Sharp, who, in an act of cool courage, had taken off in an unarmed aircraft! Another 'Nate' fell to the combined efforts of Sgts D L Clow, W J N MacIntosh and H J Meharry.

Meanwhile, Flt Lts Vanderfield and J R Kinninmont had led sections from No 21/453 Sqn aloft from Sembawang, the fighters climbing up to 20,000 ft, where they sighted a formation of Ki-48 'Lily' light bombers.

One of the fighter pilots decorated after the Malayan campaign was Plt Off Noel Sharp of No 488 Sqn, who made four claims, including two destroyed, while attached to No 243 Sqn. He scored a further victory flying Hurricanes in Java prior to be killed in action there (*RNZAF*)

Most of Sharp's victories were made flying W8138/NF-O, which the young New Zealander had had decorated with a striking Chinese Dragon motif. The fighter was destroyed at Palembang during a bombing raid on 7 February 1942 (*RNZAF*)

Diving on them, each of the section leaders shot one down. This was Vanderfield's fourth victory, whilst for Kinninmont it was the first of six claims that he would make with the Buffalo. He recalled, 'We whistled down and closed in. I picked off one of them and gave him a packet at zero range. Smoke poured from his port engine and I pulled out to watch him go down'. Kinninmont was, however, hit by return fire and he force landed back at base.

Later in the day the combined squadron escorted a mixed bomber force of RAF Blenheims, RAAF Hudsons and Dutch Glenn Martins sent to attack barges in Malaya.

The IJNAF returned in strength on the morning of 16 January when a formation of 'Nells' hit Seletar without interception. No 243 Sqn attacked some of the escorts, however, and Sgt Charlie Kronk claimed one as a probable. The CO, Sqn Ldr Frank Howell, led two sections and tried to get above the intruders in filthy weather but without success. Several hours later the enemy sent over a pair of C5M 'Babs' on a reconnaissance mission, and Howell (in his usual aircraft, W8193/WP-V) led a section aloft, sighting one of the IJNAF aircraft over Johore;

'As we broke through clouds there he was, just in front of us. We moved up into position behind him, then I let him have one good burst. The enemy immediately went straight down, bursting into flames as he went, and before he crashed one wing came off altogether. I don't think he ever knew what hit him.'

His armourer noted afterwards that in achieving his tenth, and final, victory (and only one with the Buffalo) Howell had fired just ten rounds. Mowbray Garden said admiringly that Howell was 'the complete professional. He positioned himself beautifully. Immediately he fired, his victim's starboard wing fell off and the aircraft plunged to the ground'.

As well as interceptions, the Buffalo units continued to mount bomber escort and offensive strafing sorties against the seemingly inexorable Japanese advance down the Malay Peninsula. One such mission came early on 17 January when six of the Australian Buffaloes escorted obsolete Vildebeeste biplanes sent to bomb targets on the mainland. Several of the fighters also went down to strafe.

As the Buffaloes headed back south over the Muar River, they encountered two Ki-27s and a 'Navy 0' fighter attempting to attack the Vildebeeste. All three were claimed shot down. Flying 'GA-B' (believed to have been AN180), Sgt Alf Clare destroyed one of the Ki-27s and then shared the 'Navy 0' with Doug Vanderfield. The 'Navy '0' was almost certainly the 64th Sentai Ki-43 'Oscar' flown by Lt Rokuz Kato, who was killed. His demise was Alf Clare's fifth success, so making him the first Allied pilot to achieve five victories in the Buffalo. Vanderfield also shared the probable destruction of another Ki-27 with Flt Lt Grace.

Flg Off 'Congo' Kinnimont was one of No 21 Sqn's more successful pilots, making five claims (including two destroyed) with the Buffalo. His assigned fighter, AN172/GA-S, was adorned with a boxing kangaroo as Kinnimont's personal marking. He wrote the fighter off in a crash landing at Port Swettenham on 15 December (*RAAF*)

Seen during his later service as CO of Boomerang-equipped No 5 Sqn RAAF, Sgt Alf Clare was the first pilot to become an ace flying the Buffalo (*RAAF*)

The action in the skies over Singapore continued to intensify, and shortly after the successful No 453 Sqn pilots returned to Sembawang the airfield was attacked and severely damaged by two-dozen G3Ms – several Buffaloes were also destroyed. As the bombers approached the base three Dutch Buffaloes scrambled, as did the available aircraft from No 243 Sqn. Both 'Blondie' Holder and Geoff Fisken got in amongst the enemy formation, and in an outstanding display of airmanship each pilot downed a 'Nell' and shared the destruction of two more between them, with Holder claiming a fifth bomber as a probable. These three victories took the latter pilot to 'acedom' – just a few minutes after Alf Clare had achieved this distinction. Fisken later recalled;

'That was a big day, and we had a lovely time. We came out of cloud and we were about 4000 ft above them – Navy 96 bombers – in a straggled vic formation. There was only "Blondie" Holder and I, and I thought "thank God we've got height to get some speed up". We dived down and went straight through them, firing all the way, and then came up underneath them again. On each occasion I set fire to one going down and hit another in the belly coming up. We claimed three bombers – two definitely went into the jungle – before they outdistanced us, but several others were leaving trails of smoke as they disappeared over the horizon.'

Plt Off 'Snowy' Bonham also shot down a G3M 'Nell' and claimed another probably destroyed, writing afterwards of his first success;

'Chased enemy aircraft 50 miles. Attacked 27 Type 96 Mitsubishi bombers alone. One probable, another damaged. Confirmed at a later date. Force landed at Seletar owing to rear gunners' hitting petrol tank and hydraulics, etc.'

Although there had been further damage inflicted on Singapore's airfields, on a positive note the first Hurricanes flew in formation over the city to boost morale, but later in the day the surviving Dutch Brewsters returned to Java.

UNRELENTING PRESSURE

Offensive sorties continued despite the RAF being heavily outnumbered in the air. Soon after dawn on the 18th four Buffaloes from No 21/453 Sqn escorted six Blenheims on a raid, and according to the unit's Operational Record Book, 'On returning to Sembawang enemy fighter aircraft were encountered. In the ensuing engagement, Flg Off D M Sproule downed an Army "97" single-seat fighter'. It was Daryl Sproule's first victory, and he gained another on 14 April 1943 when flying Kittyhawks over New Guinea with No 77 Sqn. Four months later, having just been made CO of this unit, he was shot down, captured and executed by the Japanese.

Over Singapore, No 488 Sqn was also soon in action on the 18th. Flt Lt *(text continues on page 64)*

No 488 Sqn's most successful pilot was Sgt Eddie Kuhn, seen here sat on the far right, who is thought to have eventually been credited with a total of five victories, three of them on the Buffalo (*RNZAF*)

COLOUR PLATES

1
F2A-1 BuNo 1393/3-F-13 of VF-3,
flown by Lt John S Thach, USS
Saratoga (CV-3), 19 March 1940

2
Buffalo I AS419 of 805 NAS,
flown by Lt R A Brabner,
Maleme, Crete, 19 March 1941

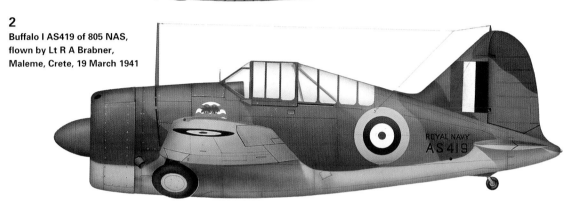

3
Buffalo I W8182/WP-Q of No 243
Sqn, flown by Sgt G B Fisken,
Kallang, Singapore, June 1941

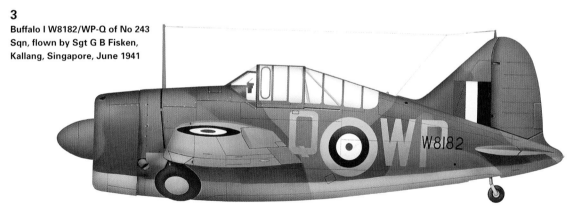

4
Brewster Model 239 BW-361/
'White 8' of 1/LLv 24, flown
by 1Lt Joel Savonen, Mikkeli,
July 1941

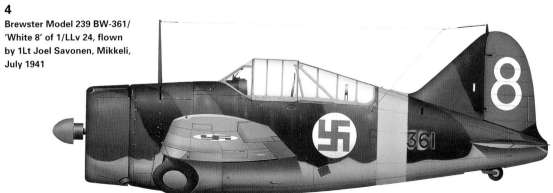

5

Brewster Model 239 BW-366/
'Orange 6' of 3/LLv 24, flown
by Capt Jorma Karhunen,
Lappeenranta, August 1941

6

Brewster Model 239 BW-383/
'Black 7' of 4/LLv 24, flown by
SSgt Martti Alho, Rantasalmi,
August 1941

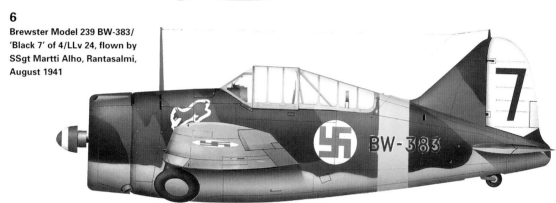

7

Brewster Model 239 BW-380/
'Black 1' of LLv 24, flown by Maj
Gustaf Magnusson, Rantasalmi,
August 1941

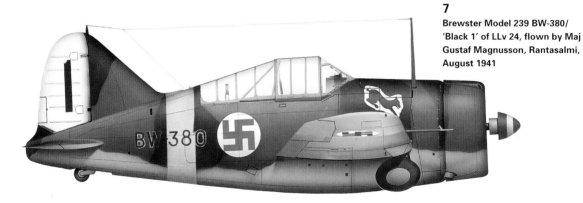

8

Brewster Model 239 BW-379/
'Orange 9' of 3/LLv 24, flown
by 1Lt Pekka Kokko, Immola,
September 1941

9
Buffalo I W8198/NF-U of No 488
Sqn RNZAF, flown by Flt Lt J N
Mackenzie, Kallang, Singapore,
October 1941-January 1942

10
Buffalo I AN196/WP-W of No 243 Sqn,
flown by Flg Off M H Holder, Kota
Bharu, Malaya, 8 December 1941

11
Buffalo I W8157/TD-M of No 453
Sqn RAAF, flown by Flt Lt T A
Vigors, Sembawang, Singapore,
10 December 1941

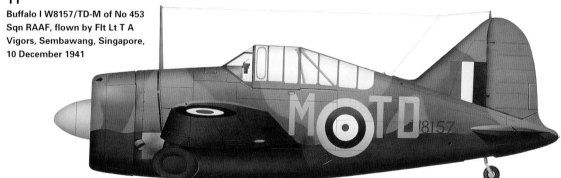

12
Buffalo I AN185/TD-V of No 453
Sqn RAAF, flown by Plt Off R D
Vanderfield, Ipoh, Malaya,
13 December 1941

13
Buffalo I W8209/TD-F of No 453
Sqn RAAF, flown by Sgt M N
Read, Ipoh, Malaya, December
1941

14
Buffalo I W8245/RD-D of No 67
Sqn, flown by Sgt G A
Williams, Mingaladon, Burma,
23 December 1941

15
Buffalo I W8243/RD-B of No 67
Sqn, flown by Sgt C V Bargh,
Mingaladon, Burma, 23
December 1941

16
Brewster Model 239 BW-351/
'White 4' of 2/LLv 24, flown by
WO Yrjö Turkka, Kontupohja,
January 1942

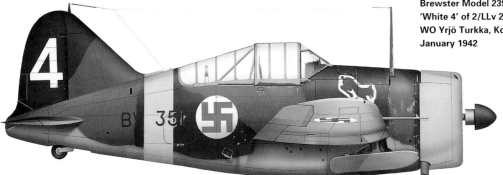

17
Buffalo I W8138/NF-O of No 488
Sqn RNZAF, flown by Plt Off N C
Sharp, Kallang, Singapore,
January 1942

18
Brewster B-339C B-3100 of
2-VIG-V ML-KNIL, flown by
Lt A G Deibel, Kallang,
Singapore, 12 January 1942

19
Buffalo I W8139/WP-B of No 243
Sqn, flown by Flt Lt M Garden,
Kallang, Singapore, 12/13
January 1942

20
Buffalo I W8193/WP-V of No 243
Sqn, flown by Sqn Ldr F J
Howell, Kallang, Singapore,
16 January 1942

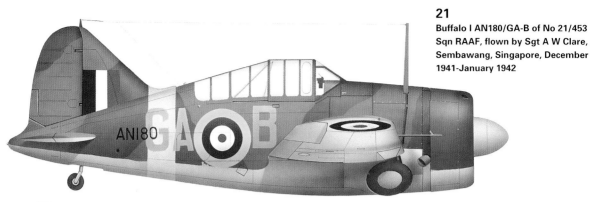

21
Buffalo I AN180/GA-B of No 21/453
Sqn RAAF, flown by Sgt A W Clare,
Sembawang, Singapore, December
1941-January 1942

22
Buffalo I W8147/WP-O of
No 243 Sqn, flown by
Sgt B S Wipiti, Kallang,
Singapore, 21 January 1942

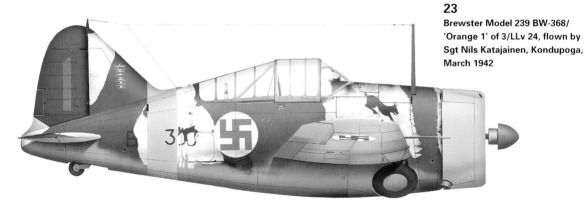

23
Brewster Model 239 BW-368/
'Orange 1' of 3/LLv 24, flown by
Sgt Nils Katajainen, Kondupoga,
March 1942

24
Brewster Model 239 BW-384/
'Orange 3' of 2/LeLv 24, flown
by 2Lt Lauri Nissinen,
Tiiksjärvi, May 1942

25
F2A-3P Buffalo BuNo 01512/
MF-17 of VMF-221, flown by
2Lt Charles M Kunz, Midway
Island, 4 June 1942

26
Brewster Model 239 BW-352/
'White 2' of 2/LeLv 24, flown
by MSgt Eero Kinnunen,
Tiiksjärvi, June 1942

27
Brewster Model 239 BW-372/
'White 5' of 2/LeLv 24, flown
by 1Lt Lauri Ohukainen,
Tiiksjärvi, June 1942

28
Brewster Model 239 BW-393/
'White 7' of 1/LeLv 24, flown by
Capt Eino Luukkanen, Römpötti,
October 1942

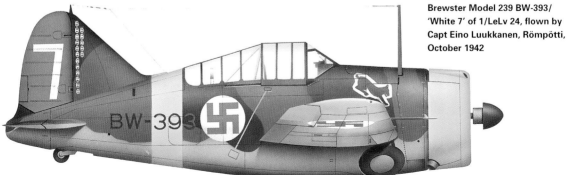

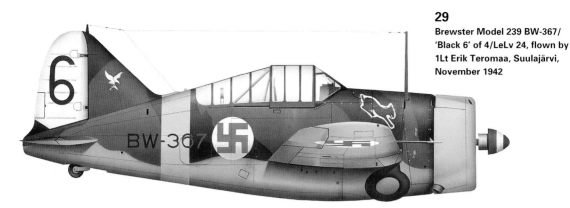

29

Brewster Model 239 BW-367/
'Black 6' of 4/LeLv 24, flown by
1Lt Erik Teromaa, Suulajärvi,
November 1942

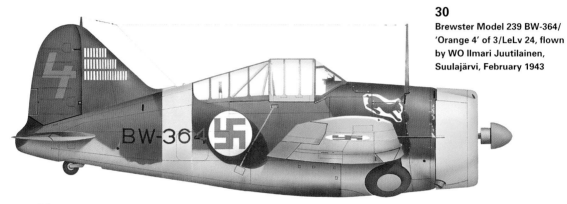

30

Brewster Model 239 BW-364/
'Orange 4' of 3/LeLv 24, flown
by WO Ilmari Juutilainen,
Suulajärvi, February 1943

31

Brewster Model 239 BW-370/
'Black 4' of 2/LeLv 24, flown by
1Lt Aulis Lumme, Suulajärvi,
May 1943

32

Brewster Model 239 BW-393/
'Orange 9' of 3/LeLv 24, flown
by 1Lt Hans Wind, Suulajärvi
September 1943

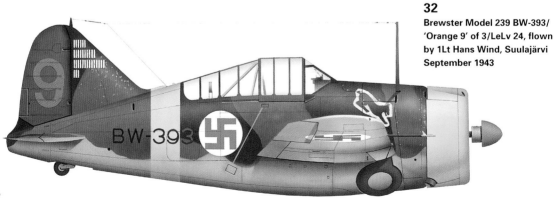

1

2

John Hutcheson claimed his only victory, while squadronmate Sgt Eddie Kuhn shot down one fighter, and possibly a second, to maintain his path to probable 'acedom'. The IJNAF did in fact lose two Zero-sens, one of which was flown by PO2c Yoshihiro Sakuraba. Three others were claimed probably destroyed.

No 243 Sqn had also scrambled at the same time as No 488 Sqn, and the unit had another day of heavy fighting. Kiwi Plt Off G L Bonham, who was jumped by a Zero-sen, noted 'Attacked fighters which turned out to be Navy 0s. Broke off attack on bombers owing to Navy 0 jumping on my tail'. Plt Off Noel Sharp, who was still on loan from No 488 Sqn, was credited with an A6M for his third, and penultimate, victory, but in the process had most of his rudder shot away. He was able to land his crippled Buffalo safely, however. Also successful was former Blenheim pilot Sgt 'Ginger' Baldwin, who also claimed an A6M destroyed, while others claimed three probables.

Several hours later, a further raid came in from the north, and a combined formation from Nos 243 and 488 Sqns scrambled once more, but this time they were hit whilst still climbing. Eddie Kuhn chased a fighter off Hutcheson's tail, although the latter was still forced to crash-land. Plt Off E W Cox of No 488 Sqn was killed and five of No 243 Sqn's Buffaloes returned with varying degrees of damage – Noel Sharp made his second emergency landing of the day. The promising Plt Off 'Snowy' Bonham was also involved in a dogfight, and he had his knee shattered by a bullet. In great pain, he managed to coax his aircraft back to a crash-landing at Kallang. Evacuated, Bonham later flew Tempests in the UK, where he downed five V1 flying bombs, including three by 'tipping'.

The action on 19 January was concentrated around Muar, on the southwest coast of Malaya, where the defenders were in desperate straits. At first light 'Congo' Kinninmont of No 21/453 Sqn led a pair of Buffaloes on a reconnaissance mission south of Malacca, where he claimed a Ki-51 'Sonia' shot down.

Shortly before 0700 hrs, eight more Australian Buffaloes escorted Wirraways and Dutch Glenn Martin bombers to Muar. Over the target they encountered a trio of Ki-51s of the 27th Sentai, led by 20-year-old 2Lt Haruo Matsuura, and one of them was immediately shot down by Flt Lt R A Kirkman. The others were pursued by Sgt K Gorringe and Flt Lt Vanderfield, who each brought one down. For Vanderfield, this was his fifth, and final, victory, thus making him the third of the Allied Buffalo pilots to attain ace status. Ki-43s of the 59th Sentai then intervened and Sgt H W Parsons was shot down and killed.

Shortly after lunch five more Buffaloes, led by Sqn Ldr Harper on one of his few operational sorties, headed back to Muar in company with aircraft from No 488 Sqn, who provided top cover. As they neared the target they were bounced by Ki-43s, who shot down two of the No 488 Sqn aircraft on their first pass. Only 'Congo' Kinninmont succeeded in fighting back, shooting down one of the 'Oscars' (identified as a Zero) near Bahu Patat.

The 20th saw Singapore suffer its heaviest raid to date when 80 bombers from the JAAF and IJNAF appeared over the island at mid-morning. The Buffaloes of Nos 243 and 488 Sqns, now reinforced by the Hurricanes of Nos 232 Sqn, were scrambled too late to intercept the raiders. Later

As well as heavy attrition in the air, the Buffalo squadrons also had to endure constant attacks on their airfields, as these blazing fighters at Kallang prove (*RNZAF*)

that same day, No 243 Sqn, again in company with No 488 Sqn, intercepted a formation of six Ki-48s that had attacked Batu Pahat. Sgt Charlie Kronk and Plt Off Noel Sharp (the latter still flying with No 243 Sqn) each claimed one bomber destroyed.

Early the following morning Flt Lt Garden led a six-aircraft sweep over the mainland, one section strafing some barges. Higher up at 22,000 ft the other section was attacked by Ki-43s and Garden's aircraft was damaged in the port wing. However, Sgt Bert Wipiti destroyed one of them, both wings being seen to come off his victim. This confirmed the Maori's second kill.

Several hours later IJNAF aircraft again appeared over Singapore when a mixed force of 50+ 'Nell' and 'Betty' bombers attacked Keppel Harbour. As well as some Hurricanes, all available Buffaloes from Nos 243 and 488 Sqns scrambled from Kallang – two of the fighters were flown by Sgts Geoff Fisken and 'Ginger' Baldwin. As ever, the defenders arrived too late, struggling to attain the enemy's height. Nevertheless, the aggressive Baldwin shot down one of the G4Ms, while Fisken also attacked the bombers and damaged a 'Betty'. Then, near Bakri, the latter pilot shot up an A6M that he initially claimed as a probable, although it was later upgraded to 'confirmed', thus giving him his fifth victory in just over a week. Fisken had become the fourth, and final, Allied pilot to attain five victories with the Buffalo.

The Japanese bombers had hit Tengah and Singapore City during the course of the day, causing further carnage and misery to the local populace. By dusk Nos 243 and 488 Sqns could muster just ten aircraft between them.

Singapore was again targeted by the IJNAF on the 22nd when 50+ bombers from the Genzan and Kanoya *Kokutais*, with fighter escorts, appeared in the late morning. The Genzan 'Nells' hit Kallang just as a quartet of No 488 Sqn Buffaloes were preparing to take off. John Mackenzie remarked 'I remember the bombs going across and past me on my right wing. It is a frightening thing when the airfield blows up almost in front of you'.

Some No 243 Sqn fighters got airborne minutes later and joined up with a handful of Hurricanes, but they were quickly engaged by the escorting Zero-sens. The Buffaloes attacked the bombers and Wipiti shot one down to claim his third victory – the only success for the Buffalo units during the course of the day. There was swift retribution from the fighter escorts, however, with Sgts Vin Arthur and the irrepressible 'Ginger' Baldwin being killed. The latter had two claims in the Buffalo to his credit, and it has been reported that he also had additional successes from his time flying Blenheim fighters, although evidence to support these victories is missing.

These losses adversely affected morale among the fighter units, and things were only going to get worse.

Over the next few days some attempt was made to support the beleaguered troops on the mainland, and when the Japanese began landing at Endau, on the east coast of Malaya, on the 26th, the only force available to oppose them were the antiquated Vildebeeste biplanes of Nos 36 and 100 Sqns and some RAAF Hudsons. The first wave departed Singapore shortly before 1400 hrs, its hurriedly assembled fighter escort including the Buffaloes of No 243 Sqn – one flight was led by Mowbray Garden. Other Buffaloes from No 21/453 Sqn covered the Hudsons.

An hour later they approached the target area in fairly clear weather and sighted the Japanese transports and landing craft just as the covering Ki-27 fighters arrived. One of them quickly damaged Garden's aircraft, although he managed to bring another 'Nate' down and then escape back to Kallang. His wingmen flew down to strafe the barges, covered by two other Buffaloes, and although they were intercepted, they all returned. Plt Off J M Cranstone claimed an A6M while Bert Wipiti was also credited with a Ki-27 destroyed – his fourth, and last, Buffalo victory, although he later achieved 'acedom' flying Spitfire IXs with No 485 Sqn in Europe during 1943. These were No 243 Sqn's final successes with the Buffalo.

No 21/453 Sqn was also in action, but in spite of the best efforts of the fighter escorts, the lumbering Vildebeestes suffered crippling losses.

Early the next day Sgts Wipiti and Kronk flew an uneventful reconnaissance mission, while in an attack on Kallang two more of No 243 Sqn's aircraft were destroyed. The unit then transferred its surviving aircraft, together with some pilots (including Fisken and Wipiti), to No 453 Sqn and disbanded. No 488 Sqn was re-equipped with Hurricanes and the remnants of No 21 Sqn embarked for Australia, leaving No 453 Sqn as the sole Buffalo unit in Singapore.

A BITTER DEFEAT

The arrival of another convoy was covered on 28 January, but the sense of isolation for the defenders of Singapore was increased when the causeway connecting the island to Malaya was blown on the 31st. The following day Sgt Geoff Fisken was in action once more, as he later described;

'By 1 February 1942 I already had five victories against various Japanese aircraft. Little did I know that this would be my last fight in the Buffalo. Pushing my nose over and picking up speed, I hurtled down at the swarm of Zeros below. I picked one out and gave him a three-second burst. With no protective armour, it burst into flames and cart wheeled down. Two of his friends latched onto me and I tried to shake them. I got a bit of cannon shell in the leg and a bullet in the arm. The Buffalo was chewed to pieces as I dove for the deck. My undercarriage was shot out and my engine was coughing and smoking as my prop stopped. I managed to bring it into Kallang, crash-landing there. I busted up my knee in the process, but other than that I was all right.

'With my arm in plaster and me walking on a stick, I wasn't much use to the RNZAF. On 12 February I and some others were loaded onto a sampan and delivered to a larger ship that took us to New Zealand.'

The Zero-sen was Fisken's sixth victory, and he thus became the most successful Allied pilot to fly the Buffalo.

With six confirmed victories, the most successful Allied Buffalo pilot was Sgt Geoff Fisken of No 243 Sqn. During a subsequent tour in the Southwest Pacific flying Kittyhawks with No 15 Sqn RNZAF, he was credited with five more victories to become the most successful Commonwealth pilot against the Japanese (*RNZAF*)

Among the Buffaloes flown by Fisken was W8134/WP-M, which was the first aircraft delivered to 'B' Flight of No 243 Sqn on 13 March 1941 (*G Fisken*)

There were a few desultory sorties made over the next few days, but conditions on the island were now virtually untenable, and by the 6th the four surviving Buffaloes had evacuated to Palembang, on Java, although groundcrews were ordered to remain and fight as infantry. The last airworthy Buffalo in Singapore flew out on the 10th with a Hurricane pilot at the controls (this was a damaged machine that had been patched up). Several injured Buffalo pilots, including Tim Vigors, escaped by sea that same day.

Singapore fell on 15 February, by which time the Dutch aircraft of VlG-V in the East Indies had also seen desultory action against the Japanese, making a number of claims but also suffering heavy losses. For example, on 24 January the Brewsters of 1-VlG-2 shot two IJNAF Zero-sens, one of which fell to the unit CO, Kapt Andrias van Rest, who had earlier been credited with a floatplane (probably an F1M 'Pete') destroyed. The second A6M fell to Lt P Benjamins. However, as in Malaya, the Dutch units were soon overwhelmed, though some of the notable pilots still continued to claim.

On 9 February the enemy raided Tjililian, and of the five Buffaloes that took off three were shot down. The remaining two did claim a Zero-sen destroyed. Six Buffaloes were still on the ground at Tjililian when the IJNAF attacked, and only one survived the raid. Thus, 2-VlG-V had almost ceased to exist. Ten days later eight Brewsters took off from Semplak to intercept a raid escorted by at least 20 A6Ms. Four of the Dutchmen were shot down, and Lt August Deibel, who had achieved some success over Malaya, had a ten-minute fight with a Zero-sen before being wounded, although he landed safely.

By 7 March only four airworthy Brewsters remained, and Kapt van Helsdingen led 2Lt Deibel with Sgts J F Scheffer and 'Tub' Bruggink to support ground troops near Kembang. Over Lembang, they encountered a Japanese fighter that was attacked by Deibel and then disappeared. The quartet later encountered some A6Ms, and in the subsequent fight Diebel was hit but managed to get down at Andir shortly before Scheffer, who was credited with a Ki-43 destroyed. Jacob van Helsdingen (in B-396) and Bruggink (in B-3107) were then attacked by more Zero-sens, and in the action that ensued van Helsdingen was credited with an A6M shot down before he was killed – this victory made him and Diebel jointly the most successful Dutch Brewster pilots. Bruggink, who had previously claimed two victories, managed to escape into a cloud and recover to Andir. The Dutch surrendered soon afterwards.

Few decorations were awarded after the Malaya campaign, although several were presented to successful Buffalo pilots. Flt Lts Mowbray Garden and John Hutcheson, Flg Off Gordon Bonham and Plt Off Noel Sharp (who was killed in Java) received DFCs, while Sgts Bert Wipiti and Eddie Kuhn were each presented with the DFM.

DEFENDERS OF BURMA

By the spring of 1941 tensions were rising between Japan and Britain over control of the latter country's various territories in the Far East. Amongst them was Burma, a vast country almost half the size of Europe. It was plainly obvious that some kind of fighter defence would be needed in the area to deter Japanese aggression, particularly against the Burmese capital Rangoon, whose port was the sea terminus for the so-called Burma Road supply route to China. This made it a key target for enemy air attack.

As in Malaya, the Air Ministry had decreed that the Buffalo would be suitable for the task of providing the aerial defence of Burma. From July 1941 crated aircraft began arriving at Mingaladon airfield, on the outskirts of Rangoon, where they were assembled by technicians of the resident unit, Blenheim-equipped No 60 Sqn. Among those who tested them was Flt Lt Bill Gill, formerly of the Burma Volunteer Air Force.

In mid-October No 67 Sqn was sent up from Singapore, and on arrival it received 16 new Buffaloes, with 14 more held in reserve. The aircraft were then assembled at a rate of about two per day so that by mid-November most had been tested, but they were soon grounded for

Personnel of No 67 Sqn's 'B' Flight gather in front of one of their newly assembled Buffaloes at Mingaladon in the autumn of 1941. Standing in the centre wearing a life jacket is Flg Off Peter Bingham-Wallis, whilst the pilot to the extreme right is Sgt Gordon Williams, who later achieved many successes. Sgt Vic Bargh, sitting on the cockpit sill, was another successful pilot (*P M Bingham-Wallis*)

checks on the Cyclone engines' valve springs. No 67 Sqn was led by Sqn Ldr R A Milward at the time, with Flt Lts Colin Pinckney and Jack Brandt as flight commanders. Amongst its pilots were several who had, or would achieve, significant success. These were Flg Off John Wigglesworth, who had five claims, including four destroyed from the Battle of Britain, and New Zealanders Sgts Vic Bargh and Gordon Williams.

Following the outbreak of hostilities in the Far East, the Japanese initially concentrated on the campaign in Malaya. However, they did commence reconnaissance flights over airfields adjacent to the Thai-Burma border, so No 67 Sqn

Sgt Gordon 'Willie' Williams was one of No 67 Sqn's most successful pilots during the Burma campaign, earning himself a DFM (*C V Bargh*)

sent detachments to advanced fields at Moulmein and along the Tenasserim Peninsula. A typical day's flying for this period took place on 15 December when Flt Lt Brandt led a section to Mergui. From here they flew some patrols, before being replaced the following day by a section led by Flt Lt Pinckney.

One of the aircraft flown to Mergui on the 16th was a camera-equipped Buffalo assigned to Flg Off Peter Bingham-Wallis. On the 19th Pinckney and Bargh escorted Bingham-Wallis on a reconnaissance mission as far as the Kra Isthmus, although all three pilots had received strict instructions not to shoot at anything! A further detachment to the south was led by Flg Off Wigglesworth. They were joined on the 21st by three more Buffaloes, led by the CO, and they made an attack on Prachuab Girikhan airfield, where Bingham-Wallis had previously seen some enemy aircraft. In No 67 Sqn's first action of the war the CO damaged one aircraft while Sgt E H Beable claimed to have destroyed an 'Army 97' and Sgt Gordon Williams two 'Navy 96 dive-bombers'.

FIRST RAID ON RANGOON

The initial lull by the enemy in Burma was soon to be shattered, however, as on 23 December the JAAF mounted its first raid against Rangoon and the surrounding airfields. Some 60+ Ki-21 'Sally' and 47 Ki-30 'Ann' bombers, escorted by 30 Ki-27 'Nate' fighters, appeared over southern Burma. Given little warning, 15 of No 67 Sqn's Buffaloes and a dozen Tomahawks of the American Volunteer Group (AVG) were scrambled and, given the circumstances, achieved good results.

Already flying on patrol at about 20,000 ft were 'Ketchil' Bargh and Gordon Williams, and they were among the first to sight the enemy armada. Bargh excitedly called over the radio, 'Hell! Showers of 'em, Look Willie! Showers of 'em!' However, both pilots, like their colleagues, was soon fighting for their lives against the nimble and well flown Ki-27s. Bargh's battle with the fighters allowed his fellow New Zealander to get

in amongst the bombers, and Williams was subsequently credited with one shot down, another probably destroyed and four more damaged. W8243/RD-B, flown by Vic Bargh, was also heavily damaged, as he recalled;

'Willie and I were up. Now it's often said that we had plenty of warning. We had no warning. We were up there patrolling because that's what we did, all the time, a pair of us. That day it just happened to be Willie and I. We saw these aeroplanes coming. We'd never seen anything like it. We said "Well here they are" on the radio, and the others started to get off the ground. All our squadron started to take-off.'

The pair then spotted 15 'Sallys' crossing them at right angles, Bargh continuing;

'I saw the bombers – I didn't see the fighters. Willie went inside me but I held back a bit to attack a bomber that was "dragging the chain". I thought "I'll nail this bugger if I can". Anyway, I missed him, and as I missed I was overtaken by all these fighters – I was surrounded by about 30 fighters I think. The first lot that came we found out were called "Nates", with fixed undercarriages. They got onto me quickly, and they could follow me round just a few feet behind my tail. I couldn't handle them, and I never fired the guns. No, they beat me. However, my

Sitting at readiness at Mingaladon in late 1941, W8243/RD-B saw action against the first major Japanese raid on Rangoon on 23 December when Sgt 'Ketchil' Bargh claimed a Ki-21 destroyed and another as a probable (*P M Bingham-Wallis*)

Also aloft on 23 December was W8245/RD-D, which was the regular aircraft of Flg Off G S Sharp but flown on this occasion by Sgt Gordon Williams. The latter avoided the fighter escort to shoot down a Japanese bombers and claim a second one as a probable (*G J Thomas*)

Twenty-year-old New Zealander Sgt 'Ketchil' Bargh achieved several successes flying Buffaloes with No 67 Sqn. Described as 'incomparable' by his flight commander, he was eventually credited with three victories and two probables (*C V Bargh*)

pursuer was too close, and his bullets ripped through the bottom of my aeroplane – I had no armour plating – before he overshot me.

'Willie, meanwhile, had gotten stuck into the bombers and shot one down. He followed the first lot of bombers and damaged quite a few others. I climbed up again, and lo and behold I saw a mob of about 15 bombers – beautiful looking things too, shining in the sun – going along. They were heading for the docks or Rangoon. I was below them and they didn't have any fighters that I could see, so I climbed up, but couldn't see very well because I'd been going flat out. With the Buffalo, when you went flat out for a while, oil would leak from the engine and smear itself all over the windscreen. I took off one of my flying boots, and it dropped into the bottom of the aeroplane because there was no floor to the cockpit. I then used my sock to clean the windscreen.'

Having calmly cleared his view, the young Kiwi returned to the fray;

'When these jokers came back from dropping their bombs I latched onto them. I was at about 17,000 ft when I attacked them. My guns wouldn't fire properly though – they'd fire four or five rounds then stop. Some guns would fire longer than others, then they'd knock off. This was going on over the Martaban Sea. I got one smoking like hell from both engines and can't understand why it didn't burst into flames, but it didn't. I pulled out and was going down towards the Sundarbans (mouths of the Irrawaddy), and I thought that I'd keep going after the ones I had.

'I was making quarter attacks, getting in behind one, firing the guns and then getting out again. I estimated that there were four bombers trailing smoke, or fuel vapour where I had punctured the tanks. Then another one pulled out of the formation, so I said "This is it, I'm going with this joker". He went down like the other one, and I followed him all the way. He didn't turn down the coast to land on a beach, however – he went straight into the low hills. The aeroplane burnt up and I photographed it.'

Bargh subsequently claimed one Ki-21 destroyed, one probable and four damaged, and although his aircraft was damaged as well, he flew two more patrols in it that afternoon, followed by another four the next day, Christmas Eve. He also commented 'The Japanese fighters were very good'.

Flg Off J F Lambert claimed a Ki-21 destroyed too, although like Flg Off John Wigglesworth he thought the 'Sallys' were He 111s – an understandable mistake, as they did bear a passing resemblance to the early-model Heinkel. The latter was credited with a probable, and wrote of his final claim, and his only one against the Japanese;

'I saw one enemy bomber about 4000 ft below me. I turned to dive on it but lost it immediately. As I was looking for this single machine for a fourth time I saw the large formation just as they dropped their bombs on our base. I chased them and did two climbing astern attacks on the port section. On the second attack the port machine broke away downwards, with white smoke coming from its starboard engine. I lost sight of him and continued attacking the rest of the formation as far as the coast east of Rangoon. My attacks had no apparent effect on them, and I returned to base when my ammunition was exhausted.'

Wigglesworth, like many other Allied pilots, also commented 'Surprised at speed of the bombers, as I was under the impression that Jap aircraft were not much good'.

Flying W8245/RD-D, Peter Bingham-Wallis chased a formation of 'Type 97' bombers northeast of Mingaladon and claimed several damaged, while Plt Off G S Sharp damaged one of the Ki-30s before being attacked by the escort. Sgt W J Christiansen also probably destroyed a 'Heinkel'. The AVG, too, made a number of claims, boosting the defenders' total to 13 bombers destroyed and seven probables. A Ki-27 was also destroyed and another listed as a probable. Rangoon had been heavily hit, however, as had Mingaladon. At the latter site a number of aircraft had also been destroyed.

Amidst all the carnage at Mingaladon, one of the No 67 Sqn groundcrew recalled that Colin Pinckney 'landed in his usual sedate way'. The nonchalant young pilot taxied to a stop and reported 'Yes, I got one, possibly two – can't be sure. Where's the char?'

In spite of all the damage, by dint of hard work the squadron had 14 aircraft ready for operations the following morning, but in the absence of another raid the squadron flew a strafing mission instead.

The aircraft in the centre of this trio of No 67 Sqn Buffaloes is thought to be W8239/RD-A. This was the machine regularly flown by Flt Lt Colin Pinckney, who undertook several successful strafing attacks on Japanese-held airfields in January 1942 (*author's collection*)

A pair of Buffaloes from No 67 Sqn claw their way into the sky during a scramble against another Japanese raid. Lacking an effective early warning system in-theatre, the unit was greatly hampered in its efforts to defend Burma from attack (*P M Bingham-Wallis*)

At about 1100 hrs on Christmas Day, the Japanese returned in even greater strength when two raids closed on Rangoon from different directions. The first numbered almost 60 Ki-21s, escorted by 25 Ki-43 'Oscars', while the second, approaching from the Tenasserim coast, consisted of eight Ki-21s, 24+ Ki-30s and an escort of 32 Ki-27s. Again, the defending Buffaloes and AVG Tomahawks had little warning of the attack, and thus were scrambled late.

Flt Lts Brandt and Pinckney each led sections of six aircraft aloft, the latter being given top cover by two more fighters flown by Peter Bingham-Wallis and Gordon Williams. Having just reached 20,000 ft, the latter pair spotted two formations of bombers. After radioing their squadronmates, telling them that they had found the enemy, the two Buffalo pilots dived on the JAAF aircraft. Williams hit one of them, which Bingham-Wallis then also went for;

'I hit the same bomber, which was trailing a stream of fuel vapour. After attacking it, the bomber fell away out of formation and crashed into the sea.'

The pair were then bounced by the escort, as Gordon Williams later recounted;

'I saw a fighter dead ahead and fired at its tail section, sending the machine spiralling down out of control. It appeared as if the pilot had been hit. I had no time to see if the aircraft crashed, as bullet holes started to appear through my own starboard wing.'

Colin Pinckney, who was flying W8144/RD-C, also witnessed this fight, before becoming engaged with the enemy himself;

'The flight passed under a formation of bombers that were 2000 ft above us shortly after they had hit Rangoon. I saw two weaving aircraft (Bingham-Wallis and Williams) attack these bombers, and several Japanese fighters were flying behind them. I turned to pursue the bombers but then saw a larger force over Mingaladon and started climbing to a position on the sunward side of them.

'As we climbed, I was told on the R/T by "Red 4" that there was a fighter on my tail. I turned sharply to port over "Red 2", and as I was taking evasive action I saw a Japanese fighter firing at a Buffalo – almost certainly "Red 2" – away on the starboard side. I fired a short burst at it and the fighter disappeared under my wing. I was then attacked again, and after making a complete aileron turn I saw a Buffalo gliding away to the north with white smoke trailing from its engine. I assumed that the pilot would make a normal forced landing. I was then attacked again, this time by two fighters, and got a good burst at one.'

Pinckney was correct in his identification of 'Red 2', but Sgt John Macpherson crashed and was killed. The rest of his flight were also engaged, including the irrepressible 'Ketchil' Bargh, who had an exhausting 20-minute fight with a Ki-27 that he eventually claimed as a probable;

'There were six of us up in the second battle and five were shot down, four being killed, but I didn't get hit. One of the Japs attacked me from the side. I was weaving, which was the thing to do. There was a swarm of Japanese fighters – you couldn't see for the damned things above us – and when my opponent attacked me I dived right away. When I came up again, as I had done a couple of days before, I couldn't see any Japanese aircraft at all. I had missed them. But the others were all shot down. I reckon it was a damned foolish day.'

Bargh had been set upon by a Ki-43, although as he described above, he eventually evaded his pursuer by diving for the deck – a favoured evasive technique for Buffalo pilots. He noted in his log book;

'Patrol. One Army 97 fighter probable. Attacked by 30 fighters. Bombs dropped on Rangoon and Mingaladon. Ted Hewitt, Ron McNabb, John Lambert and Jack Macpherson shot down and killed.'

Bargh also noted that the escorts had retractable undercarriages, and like his colleagues in Malaya, he had discovered an uncomfortable truth;

'There was no British or American fighter ever built that could dogfight with the Japanese. You had to use other tactics – come in from above, or at the same level at the very least, then dive away before they got onto you, because if they did get onto you, well, you were shot down.'

On Christmas Day, the Buffaloes had generally come off second best when dogfighting with their counterparts in the JAAF. Aside from the four No 67 Sqn fighters that had been destroyed, several others had been badly shot up. In return, the unit claimed one bomber and three fighters destroyed, with more as probables and damaged. Again, the AVG made a significant number of claims too. The 12th Sentai had indeed lost three Ki-21s over the target, and a fourth was badly hit and later force-landed. Other bombers in the formation were also damaged, as were several from the 60th Sentai that attacked after the initial wave, although none were actually lost.

The escorts had also experienced some losses in the numerous dogfights that they had fought whilst protecting the bombers, the 64th Sentai having two Ki-43s shot down – one of these was claimed by Jack Brandt. The 77th Sentai lost the Ki-27s flown by Lt Masashi Someya, who was killed, and Sgt Maj Kontetu Ri, who was taken prisoner. However, in spite of the defenders' best efforts, both Rangoon and Mingaladon had again been heavily bombed, leaving the city in chaos.

As in Malaya and Singapore, effective Japanese attacks on Allied airfields dealt a major blow to the defenders. Here, smoke billows from Mingaladon after one of the myriad attacks launched against the base by the JAAF in January 1942 (*W J Storey*)

Although there continued to be sporadic air action, little came the way of No 67 Sqn for the next ten days. The JAAF returned to Mingaladon once again on 4 January, although on this occasion only the AVG managed to intercept the enemy aircraft. Another raid was made the following day.

In spite of the need to defend Rangoon, No 67 Sqn was also called on to provide senior Army officers with crucial photographic intelligence that allowed them to assess the enemy's intentions in respect to the impending invasion of Burma.

No 67 Sqn's next action came on 9 January when, in company with AVG Tomahawks, it strafed Raheng airfield, in Thailand. Buffalo pilots claimed two 'Type 97' bombers destroyed on the ground, with one being credited to Pinckney and the other to his CO, the recently appointed Jack Brandt. Rangoon was bombed that night in retaliation, and Bingham-Wallis unsuccessfully attempted an interception. The following morning the CO led four aircraft in an attack on Mesoht airfield, in Thailand, where two Ki-30s were destroyed. Despite these strafing missions, Japanese night raids on Rangoon and other Allied airfields continued unabated.

Plt Off Paul Brewer (in W8229) added a Ki-15 'Babs' reconnaissance aircraft to No 67 Sqn's tally of victories on the 13th whilst patrolling over Tavoy. His first burst may have killed the observer, as there was no return fire, and no evasive action was taken before the enemy aircraft caught fire and crashed into the hills. The following day, during a strafing attack on Mesoht, Colin Pinckney (in W8239) attacked a Japanese transport that he identified as a 'Ju 52' on the ground as it was taxiing, leaving it in flames. Similar strafing attacks were flown during the succeeding days. On the 13th, however, No 67 Sqn began dispersing aircraft to Zayatkwin in an attempt to prevent further losses on the ground.

Ominously, on 18 January Japanese troops began to advance into Burma, and so No 67 Sqn's Buffaloes began escorting RAF bombers charged with hindering the advance. The enemy also attacked Allied airfields, and on the 20th both Brewer and Sgt John Finn were killed as they gallantly took off from Moulmein to engage Ki-27s that were strafing the base.

Three days later the first Hurricanes arrived at Mingaladon just as a wave of Ki-27s of the 50th Sentai commenced an attack on the airfield. Already airborne was 23-year-old Flt Lt Colin Pinckney in W8239, who was on a patrol with Sgt Christiansen in W8203. Wading into the waspish 'Nates', the pair became embroiled in a one-sided dogfight in which Christiansen claimed one shot down but Pinckney was overwhelmed and killed. No 67 Sqn mechanic J Helsdon Thomas wrote of the evident respect and admiration felt for the young pilot;

'"Pinckers" the unflappable, "Pinckers" the indestructible. The Japs sneaked a fighter across Mingaladon. "Pinckers" and a Sergeant pilot gave chase not knowing it was a decoy. They ran into seven Jap fighters and Pinckney, realising the situation was hopeless, told his companion to beat the hell out of it. Colin Pinckney went down, taking three Japs with him. I suppose it could be said of him that he gave his life for his friend.'

If this description of this gallant final combat is accurate then Flt Lt Colin Pinckney thus became the only pilot to achieve 'acedom' flying a Buffalo over Burma.

Although of poor quality, this is one of the few photographs available of Flt Lt Colin Pinckney. Educated at Eton and Cambridge, he had flown Spitfires with distinction during the Battle of Britain. In the chaos of Burma his final score is uncertain, but there is evidence to suggest that Pinckney became the only pilot to 'make ace' flying the Buffalo in the Burma campaign (*M Goodman*)

The day after Pinckney's demise Sqn Ldr Brandt led five of the steadily reducing number of Buffaloes in an attack on a formation of bombers he had spotted below them, and Sgt E L Sadler combined with two others to bring one of the aircraft down. A second bomber blew up when hit by a burst of fire from Plt Off A A Cooper. Finally, Sgt Vic Bargh was also involved in the action, claiming his second victory, and last on the Buffalo;

'There were seven aircraft, and four of us were trying to catch up with the buggers. We were just a bit low. We saw Hurricanes shoot down two for a certainty – you could see the bullets firing into the Japanese aeroplanes. Anyway, one went down vertically. Watching this going down, I couldn't believe it. He never even looked like pulling out. He just went straight into the ground. When I looked up, there were only four bombers left. I was flat out. I couldn't do anything more. I was cutting them off, as they had to go round in a big turn to head in the direction of home, so I was cutting across with the other blokes.

'I eventually got in behind a bomber, and its wing and engine parted from the fuselage under the weight of my fire. The machine went down like a sycamore, and I naturally claimed it destroyed. Anyway, I later went out to examine the wreck on foot, as I knew that it had crashed alongside Pegu airfield. I took some photographs.'

These are thought to have been the last victories claimed by the Buffalo during the Burma campaign. The Hurricanes mentioned had been flown by Sqn Ldrs 'Bunny' Stone and Jimmy Elsdon, COs of Nos 17 and 136 Sqns respectively.

JAAF fighters had by now all but secured air superiority over the Rangoon airfields, and with the situation on the ground rapidly deteriorating, so too did the amount of available air support. In early February No 67 Sqn withdrew north to Toungoo, from where on the 6th Flg Off John Wigglesworth led a section off for a reconnaissance mission to Cheingmai. However, as he became airborne the engine of W8213 failed and he force landed. Tragically, the fighter overturned and Wigglesworth was killed – a particularly sad end for a gifted pilot.

Sgt Bargh also flew from Toungoo, escorting Lysanders charged with flying increasingly desperate ground attack missions against enemy forces as they approached the Sittang – the last river barrier before Rangoon. On 13 February the squadron's eight surviving Buffaloes moved 200 miles further north to Magwe, from where further reconnaissance missions were flown in support of the Army.

By now more Hurricanes had arrived in Burma, allowing some No 67 Sqn pilots to make the switch to the more modern British fighter. The Buffaloes still fought on though, and on 5 March Flt Lt Bingham-Wallis led a quartet of them as escorts for a strafing attack by Hurricanes and Blenheims on the JAAF base at Chieng Mai, in northeastern Thailand.

One of No 67 Sqn's final victories of the Burma campaign was claimed by 'Ketchil' Bargh when he shot the wing off a bomber (possibly a Ki-21) to claim his second kill. He managed to locate the wreckage and have this souvenir photograph taken with it (*C V Bargh*)

Three days later Rangoon fell, thus changing the Allied situation in Burma at a stroke. With so few Buffaloes surviving, it was decided to withdraw No 67 Sqn to India to re-equip, so on the 11th the four airworthy aircraft were flown to Akyab and then on to Dum Dum, in Calcutta, by Sqn Ldr Brandt, Flg Off Geoff Sharp and Sgts Ken Rutherford and Vic Bargh. Two more followed, the last being flown out of Akyab by Flt Lt Bill Gill. The remaining pilots were evacuated by air transport.

The Buffaloes' part in the defence of Burma was over. As in Malaya, although flown with great gallantry – and no little skill – the inherent weaknesses of the Brewster had once again been cruelly exposed, and it had proved no match for the nimble Japanese fighters. Nonetheless, No 67 Sqn had claimed 27 Japanese aircraft destroyed. Only eight Buffaloes had in fact been were shot down during the campaign in Burma, resulting in the deaths of Sgts P T Cutfield, E B Hewitt, J G Finn, J Macpherson, Flg Offs P M Brewer, J F Lambert and J S Wigglesworth and Flt Lt D J C Pinckney.

Throughout the disastrous campaign in Burma No 67 Sqn had fought well, but by the end of March it had virtually ceased to exist as a fighting unit. Like in Malaya, relatively few decorations were awarded, but DFCs were promulgated for Sqn Ldr Brandt and Flt Lt Pinckney, while a well-earned DFM went to Sgt Gordon Williams.

In India No 67 Sqn began to re-equip with Hurricanes as new fighter squadrons were formed with whatever equipment was available. One of the latter was No 146 Sqn, which in early April acquired two of the six Buffaloes that had made it out of Burma. Towards the end of the month one of them, W8250, was regularly flown by the unit CO, Battle of Britain ace Sqn Ldr Count Manfred Czernin. However, the tired Brewsters were swiftly relegated to fighter training duties with No 151 Operational Training Unit, where, amongst others, future ace Flg Off Hedley Everard flew the type, which gradually faded from the scene with little pomp or ceremony.

Decorated with a small 'kiwi' motif forward of the cockpit, a mud-spattered W8245/RD-D is prepared for flight, apparently at Magwe. This photograph may have been taken after No 67 Sqn evacuated here from Mingaladon (*G J Thomas*)

FINALE OVER LAND AND SEA

As the F2A was withdrawn from US Navy service in 1941, many found employment as advanced trainers. The biggest user was Naval Air Station (NAS) New York, in Brooklyn, which at one stage had 37 F2A-3s on strength. Other users included NAS Miami, known simply as the Operational Training Unit Miami, and the Carrier Advanced Training Group, Pacific.

With the fighter now destined only for use as a trainer with the US Navy, Brewster modified the last F2A-3s on the production line through the fitment of pneumatic tail wheel tyres and a detachable gun camera mounted on the starboard forward fuselage. Both additions made the aircraft more suited to the training role.

Among a number of future aces who trained on the F2A at Miami was Ens Don 'Flash' Gordon, who subsequently claimed five kills flying Wildcat and Hellcat with VF-10. He flew 25 hours in the Brewster during training, and he recalled his experiences with the machine especially for this volume;

'I undertook my advanced training in Miami, Florida, in January-February 1942. I was excited to have been selected to fly the F2A instead of the F3F. I know it was a thrill to get out of the SNJ trainer. We were properly briefed, and cautioned about the Brewster's characteristics. It had no strange tendencies, although it would ground loop in a crosswind. I flew familiarisation and formation sorties, and was also introduced to basic fighter tactics. I did not do any weapons work. I had no problems flying the Brewster, but during our first formation flights, after familiarisation, my instructor, Lt Bill Harrison, whacked the throttle off. The other wingman and I scooted past him pronto, so we learned in a moment that the aircraft did not have aerodynamic drag! In conclusion, I think that the F2A was lighter in the air than the F4F and seemed to have more manoeuvrability, but I would not have traded it for the Wildcat! My last flight in the F2A was on 6 February 1942.'

Another pilot that later 'made ace' with nine kills in F4Fs and F6Fs was E L 'Whitey' Feightner, who flew the Buffalo from Cabanas Field, Texas;

'It was a nice aeroplane, but very underpowered. It had a curious arrangement whereby the pilot was to use the "dike", which was slang for a pair of wire cutters, that were kept in the cockpit if the F2A's notorious landing gear did not come down. The pilot could snip the cables holding them up and they would drop via gravity!'

As Feightner has intimated, training accidents were commonplace, and by 1943 there were few F2As left. Those remaining were scrapped in early 1944.

When the US Navy decided to transfer its Brewsters to advanced training units, a number of surplus airframes were passed on to the

F2A-3 '2-MF-13' of VMF-212 sits in a camouflaged revetment at Ewa Field, Hawaii, on 25 April 1942, soon after the unit had formed. It saw no action with the F2A (US Navy)

US Marine Corps. Amongst the squadrons to receive them was VMF-221, which formed at San Diego on 11 July 1941. Following the attack on Pearl Harbour five months later, the unit was embarked in *Saratoga* and despatched to remote Wake Island, in the western Pacific. However, with the island's capture the squadron was diverted north to Midway Island instead, where its 14 F2As arrived on Christmas Day. Under the command of Maj V J McCaul, VMF-221 became part of Marine Air Group 22 on 1 March, and that same day VMF-212 was formed at Marine Corps Air Station (MCAS) Ewa, on Hawaii, also with F2As.

The combat debut for the US Marine Corps' Brewsters came soon afterwards when, on 10 March, a pair of H8K4 'Mavis' flying boats left Wotje Atoll, in the Marshall Islands, and one of them headed for Midway. This aircraft was subsequently detected by radar 45 miles west of Midway and a dozen F2As, led by Capt Robert M Haynes, were vectored out to intercept the intruder. One section of four, led by Capt James L Neefus, who was flying BuNo 01537/221-MF-1, caught the 'Mavis' at 10,000 ft. After several firing passes, the four-engined flying boat went down. The F2A's first kill in US service was credited to Neefus. However, the action was not one sided, as the unit's war diary recorded;

'Marine Gunner Dickey made a tail approach and received a wound in his left shoulder and seven bullet holes in his aeroplane. This aircraft will need an engine change.'

At the end of the month eight more F2A-3s were delivered to the unit, along with some additional pilots. One of the latter was 2Lt Charles M Kunz who, on the 30th, performed his first familiarisation flight in BuNo 01550. By late May the squadron had been augmented with the arrival of additional aircraft to the extent that VMF-221 now boasted 21 F2A-3s and seven F4Fs on strength, the latter having been delivered on 26 May aboard the aircraft transport vessel USS *Kitty Hawk* (AKV-1)

The 'Mavis' claimed by VMF-221 was almost certainly conducting long-range reconnaissance ahead of a major operation by the Imperial Japanese Navy aimed at seizing Midway. The campaign opened early on 4 June when Adm Chuichi Nagumo's four aircraft carriers launched 100+ aircraft in a strike against the tiny island. The raid was detected by radar northwest of Midway at a range of 90 miles shortly before 0600 hrs. VMF-221 was led aloft by its new CO, Maj Floyd B Parks, and Capt Kirk Armistead, 21 F2As and seven F4Fs being scrambled in five divisions.

Some 15 minutes after taking off, when the fighters were about 30 miles from Midway at 14,000 ft, Parks spotted a large formation of D3A 'Val' dive-bombers and their Zero-sen escorts. His divisions engaged, but the Brewsters were overwhelmed and only three survived, including Capt

Phillip White, who shot down a 'Val' and damaged another. Ten minutes later the group led by Armistead arrived and fared little better, although they did make a number of claims before being overwhelmed and suffering significant losses. The F4F pilots claimed a total of six enemy aircraft destroyed, while Capt William Hubberd shot down a B5N 'Kate' and a Zero-sen and 2Lt Charles Kunz was credited with a pair of 'Vals' – both men were in F2As.

This F2A-3, seen in the spring of 1942 before the red in the US markings was deleted, appears to wear the code 'MF-17'. If so, then this is BuNo 1521 of VMF-221, which was the machine flown on 4 June by 2Lt Charles Kunz in action against the Japanese off Midway, when he shot down two D3A 'Val' dive-bombers (*Peter Mersky*)

Flying BuNo 01521/MF-17, Charles Kunz's kills made him the only American ace to claim victories with the F2A – he would score six kills in F4F-4s with VMF-224 over Guadalcanal later that same year. Kunz recalled the clash off Midway in his combat report;

'Our division was in the air at 0602 hrs when the radar vectored us out on a heading of 320 degrees. We climbed at almost full throttle and sighted about 40 enemy machines in five- to nine-aeroplane divisions. Shortly after reaching 17,000 ft, I saw Capt Armistead make his attack, followed by my leader, Capt Humberd. My attack was a high-speed overhead approach. I was firing at the fifth machine in the last division, and spotted two aeroplanes in flames in the fifth division that had very likely been hit by Armistead and Humberd.

'It is my belief that Lt Sandoval was drawn flat in his approach and was shot down by an enemy back seat gunner.

'I saw my target burst into flames and pull out of its formation.

'After the initial attack our division was completely separated, and I zoomed up on the starboard side of the enemy Aichi Type 99 dive-bomber formation. I was about 2000 ft above the formation when I made my second attack. Using my superior height, I attacked the dive-bomber on the port side of a vee, frequently firing short bursts until my target caught fire. The pilot then pulled out of formation to apparently let the aeroplane that was on fire alongside him get out. I kept firing short bursts at long range at the aeroplane that I had forced out of formation.

'At this point I came under attack myself, and I shoved my aeroplane over into a dive from an altitude of about 9000 ft in an effort to shake off the fighter on my tail. Levelling out just 20 ft above the water, I then made a series of radical turns in the hope that my foe couldn't get steadied on me. I glanced out of the rear and saw that it was a Zero-sen navy fighter. I continued to weave wildly at full throttle, at which point I was hit in the head by a glancing bullet. After firing a few more short bursts, the Zero-sen left.

'My aeroplane was badly shot up, and I knew that it could not be used in another attack due to the radio having been destroyed and the hydraulic system shot out. I flew for 10 or 15 minutes on a heading for Midway and circled until 0730 hrs, at which time I came in to the island and made my proper identifying approach and landed at 0750 hrs. I was

Twenty-two-year-old 2Lt Charles Kunz was the only American ace to make a claim with the F2A when, during VMF-221's disastrous engagement off Midway on 4 June 1942, he shot down two dive-bombers but was wounded by the escorting Zero-sens (*US Navy via Mrs Grace Kunz*)

Surviving pilots from the Battle of Midway at Ewa Field, Hawaii, on 22 June 1942. All but one are members of VMF-221. They are, from left to right, Capt Marion E Carl, Capt Kirk Armistead, Maj Raymond Scollin (MAG-22), Capt Herbert T Merrill, 2Lts Charles M Kunz, Charles S Hughes and Hyde Phillips, Capt Philip R White and 2Lt Roy A Corry Jr (*US Navy*)

very dizzy due to my head wound, so I immediately went off to the dispensary for treatment.

'I had expended 312 rounds from three of my guns.

'In my opinion the Zero-sen fighter has been far underestimated. I think it is probably one of the finest fighters in the present war.'

Kunz recorded in his flying logbook, 'F2A-3 01521. Combat with enemy (two bombers) Aichi Type 99'. It was his final flight in a Buffalo. This was also the last occasion that the F2A saw combat in American or Allied hands. The poor performance of the F2A-3 on 4 June 1942 led to considerable criticism of the aircraft, VMF-221's Capt Phillip White being quoted in the press as saying, 'It is my belief that any commander that orders pilots out for combat in an F2A-3 should consider the pilot as lost before leaving the ground'!

For its gallant actions during the Battle of Midway, VMF-221 was awarded a Presidential Unit Citation, but it had made a huge sacrifice – a dozen F2As and two F4Fs were lost with their pilots, and four others were wounded. Nevertheless, actions later in the day turned Midway into a decisive victory for the Americans.

After Midway, the F2A was relegated to training duties, this F2A-3 being flown on just such a sortie in August 1942 by Lt Cdr Joe Clifton. Although not an ace, Clifton was a colourful character and an icon of US Navy fighter pilots in World War 2 (*US Navy*)

Sitting in the cockpit of an F2A-3 at NAS Miami in April 1943, Lt Walter Haas explains the cockpit drills to student pilots. Haas was credited with four plus two shared victories flying F4Fs in the Pacific during 1942 (*US Navy*)

ANTIPODEAN FINALE

With the imminent fall of the Netherlands East Indies to the Japanese, in early 1942 the Dutch order for B-439s was diverted to Australia. Arriving in their factory-applied Dutch camouflage and markings, the aircraft were initially acquired by the USAAF in Australia, which used four of them. The balance was passed to the RAAF, which was itself desperately short of fighters. Some were subsequently used by the photo-reconnaissance unit at Darwin, where one was destroyed by enemy action on 29 October.

Two months earlier, nine had been delivered to Perth-based No 25 Sqn, commanded by Sqn Ldr F H Williams. For a time they constituted the sole fighter defence for both Perth and the nearby port of Fremantle. The Brewster's time in Perth was relatively uneventful, although on 30 December four aircraft were detached to Broome and Derby, in the northwest of Western Australia, for shipping protection duties. A typical sortie was performed on New Year's Day 1943 when, flying A51-10, Plt Off Mitchell provided fighter escort to the SS *Chunking*.

On 15 February No 25 Sqn's 'C' Flight became the cadre of the newly formed No 85 Sqn, led by Sqn Ldr H C N Daly. The aircrafts' days were numbered, however, and on 30 April 11 Boomerangs arrived in Western Australia. The Buffaloes had all been retired by mid-May, so ending the type's frontline service with the Western Allies.

The Buffaloes' operational swansong with the Allies was with the RAAF. Ex-Dutch B-439 A51-15 still retains its USAAF markings after being transferred to No 25 Sqn RAAF in Perth, Western Australia. In a strange touch of irony, the fighter was flown on one of its final operational sorties in early January 1943 by Flt Lt H V Montefiore, who had claimed the type's first victory on 9 December 1941 when assigned to No 21 Sqn RAAF (*RAAF*)

FINAL VICTORY

The Finnish Brewsters gained a new lease of life during the Soviet summer offensive of 1944, which is usually referred to as the 'Great Attack'. The fighters had been passed to HLeLv 26 earlier in the year, the unit having previously flown Italian Fiat G.50s.

During the first days of the offensive Soviet air force units flew more than 1000 sorties per day, with the *Shturmoviks* concentrating on breaching frontline fortifications, while the bombers attacked transport and supply infrastructure to the rear. HLeLv 26 fielded 18 Brewsters in two flights to protect the rear defences, and although obsolete for use over the frontline, their reputation as a stable gun platform with heavy armament still made them effective against bombers.

During the Soviet summer offensive HLeLv 26 was credited with 21 aircraft shot down, 1st Flight leader, and ace, 1Lt Erik Teromaa claiming four kills and 2Lt Aarno Juurinen three. The squadron lost four Brewsters and two pilots in combat, however.

By mid-July the Finns had succeeded in halting the Soviet advance and negotiated a ceasefire that became effective on 4 September. One of the terms of the Armistice was that their erstwhile German allies had to be driven out of northern Finland. As this could not be achieved within the deadline the Finns declared war on Germany, and a brief conflict known as the Lapland War began. At first both sides just kept a wary eye on each other, but Soviet pressure demanded the Finns take more robust action.

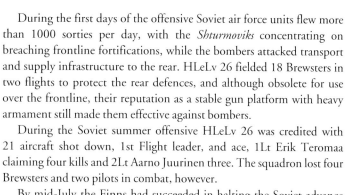

In the Finnish sector the Luftwaffe had a *Staffel* of Ju 87D Stuka dive-bombers and a half-*Staffel* of Bf 109G-6 fighters at Rovaniemi. Military operations against the Germans began on 2 October, and the only clashes with the Luftwaffe took place the following day. HLeLv 26's 1Lt Erik Teromaa and his flight flew to Oulu, from where one section of eight aircraft continued south along the coast. They were heading for the Bay of Bothnia to escort a Finnish convoy transporting troops to a landing at Tornio.

1/HLeLv 26 flight leader and future 19-kill ace 1Lt Erik Teromaa poses with BW-361 at Käkisalmi on 26 June 1944. Teromaa scored the very last Brewster victory on 3 October 1944 when he claimed a Luftwaffe Ju 87D shot down over Lapland (*O Riekki*)

The Brewsters met a formation of Stukas that were also heading for the ships, and in the one-sided battle that ensued two of the Ju 87s were shot down and three left the area damaged and trailing smoke. Teromaa, who was flying BW-361, reported;

'As I was leading a reconnaissance flight of eight BWs along the Kemi-Rovaniemi road we ran into 12 southbound Ju 87s. At first we wondered whether to fight, but as the Stukas opened fire on us we decided to engage them. I fired at the far wingman whose engine began to smoke. The aircraft then broke formation and ultimately crash-landed in a swamp between Ristijärvi and Louejärvi. SSgt Oiva Hietala saw the Stuka crash. One aeroplane fired at me and I was hit in the fuel tank. An explosive bullet also hit the cockpit, shrapnel slightly wounding me in my hand and thigh. After this I fired at another Ju 87 but saw no results. The Stukas dropped their bombs as we attacked them. They held

formation very well throughout the battle, the machine gunners targeting us with concentrated, accurate, defensive fire.'

Hietala was credited with shooting down the second Stuka to fall to the unit, and these two claims were the last ones to be made by Brewster pilots in World War 2. It was also the last combat for the Finnish fighter force, as the Soviet main offensive commenced shortly thereafter and all remaining Luftwaffe units in Finland were transferred permanently to the Eastern front.

The Brewster Model 239s had claimed 482 aerial victories with the Finnish Air Force – an outstanding score for a type that the Americans had declared totally unsuitable for military operations after the disaster at Midway in June 1942. However, the F2A-3 was 1500 lbs heavier than the Model 239 used by the Finns, and most of the Finnish pilots assigned to the Brewster in 1941 were already combat experienced from the Winter War in 1939-40, many having flown more than 100 missions. Indeed, a few of them were already aces. The Finns also boasted high levels of combat training, motivation, tactical awareness and leadership.

Brewster flying in Finland ceased on 23 January 1945 and all surviving aircraft were placed into storage as required by the flying ban issued by the Allied Supervision Commission. However, the Brewster story did not quite end there as on 2 August 1945 the type flew again when the air depot released an aircraft for liaison duties with the Air Force Headquarters. During the autumn the Staff Flight received two more Brewsters, followed by another four in 1946 – two of them were subsequently written off that same year in landing accidents. The five remaining Brewsters flew until the autumn of 1948, when they were returned to storage, the last flights of the type being performed by BW-377 and BW-382 on 14 September 1948. They were all scrapped in 1953.

Post-war, surviving Finnish Brewsters were used as 'hacks'. One such machine was BW-382 of the Air Force Headquarters Staff Flight, which is seen here paying a visit to Pori in the autumn of 1947. All Model 239s were scrapped in 1953 (*E Jaakkola*)

VALEDICTION

Although it saw conspicuous success over Finland, the Brewster fighter is probably best remembered for its inadequacies in combat. It is perhaps appropriate, therefore, to close with the words of the most successful Buffalo pilot to fly against the Japanese, Geoff Fisken. 'If only I had had an aeroplane with more horsepower. Then, maybe, I could have done some good'.

APPENDICES

Finnish Brewster Model 239 Aces

Name	Rank	Unit	Brewster score	Total score	Notes
H H Wind	Capt	3/LeLv 24	39	75	MHR (MHR twice)
E I Juutilainen	WO	3/LeLv 24	34	94	MHR (MHR twice)
J Karhunen	Capt	3/LeLv 24	25.5	31.5	MHR
L V Nissinen	1Lt	3/LeLv 24	22.5	32.5	MHR (KIA 17/6/44)
E Kinnunen	WO	2/LeLv 24	19	22.5	KIA 21/4/43
N E Katajainen	MSgt	3/LeLv 24	17.5	34.5	MHR
E A Luukkanen	Capt	1/LeLv 24	14.5	54	(MHR)
M A Alho	MSgt	4/LeLv 24	13.5	13.5	KIFA 5/6/43
E U Teromaa	1Lt	HLeLv 26	13	19	
L O Pekuri	1Lt	2/LeLv 24	12.5	18.5	(PoW 17/6/44)
K A Lumme	1Lt	4/LeLv 24	11.5	16.5	
E O Vesa	SSgt	3/LeLv 24	10.5	30.5	
I V Törrönen	Capt	4/LeLv 24	10	11	KIA 2/5/43
P J Kokko	1Lt	3/LeLv 24	10	13.5	(KIFA 19/2/44)
Y O Turkka	WO	2/LeLv 24	10	17.5	
J A Huotari	MSgt	3/LeLv 24	9.5	17.5	
T T Järvi	SSgt	2/LeLv 24	9.5	25.5	
V Pyötsiä	WO	1/LeLv 24	8.5	21.5	
J A Savonen	1Lt	1/LeLv 24	8	9	
P E Sovelius	Capt	4/LeLv 24	7	15	
L Ahokas	SSgt	3/LeLv 24	7	12	
E I Peltola	SSgt	2/LeLv 24	7	11	(KIA 2/4/44)
U K Sarjamo	1Lt	2/LeLv 24	6.5	10.5	(KIA 17/6/44)
E J Riihikallio	2Lt	2/LeLv 24	6.5	16.5	
V I Kauppinen	SSgt	3/LeLv 24	6.5	7.5	
K K Metsola	1Lt	1/LeLv 24	6	10	
H O Lampi	2Lt	2/LeLv 24	6	14	
O I Avikainen	Sgt	2/LeLv 24	6	6	
M J Salovaara	1Lt	3/LeLv 24	5.5	5.5	(KIFA 12/5/44)
O K Puro	2Lt	2/LeLv 24	5.5	33	
P K Mellin	Sgt	3/LeLv 24	5.5	5.5	PoW 9/3/42
O K Kauppinen	1Lt	3/LeLv 24	5	5	
V M Lakio	1Lt	1/LeLv 24	5	5	
K K Lindberg	1Lt	1/LeLv 24	5	5	
M Pasila	2Lt	1/LeLv 24	5	9	
J K Saarinen	2Lt	2/LeLv 24	5	23	(KIA 18/7/44)

Finnish Aces with Brewster Model 239 victories

Name	Rank	Unit	Brewster score	Total score	Notes
V I Suhonen	1Lt	1/LeLv 24	4.5	19.5	
V J Rimminen	WO	1/LeLv 24	4.5	6	
J K Sarvanto	Capt	1/LeLv 24	4	17	
H S Ikonen	MSgt	4/LeLv 24	4	6.5	
U A Nieminen	Capt	3/LeLv 26	2	11	
A I Laitinen	2Lt	3/LeLv 24	2	10	(PoW 29/6/44)
E E Lyly	Sgt	3/LeLv 24	2	8	
G E Magnusson	Maj	E/LeLv 24	1.5	5.5	(MHR)
V N Pokela	1Lt	2/LeLv 24	1	5	
N R Trontti	1Lt	HLeLv 26	1	6	(PoW 26/6/44)
A K Tervo	2Lt	1/LeLv 24	0.5	21.25	(KIA 20/8/43)

Notes
The rank shown is the one held at the time of the pilot's last claim. The unit stated is where the majority of the pilot's Brewster victories were scored. Notes mentioned in parenthesis refer to another unit or a later period. In some instances the victory totals listed here differ slightly from those published in *Osprey Aircraft of the Aces 23 - Finnish Aces of World War 2* (1998) and *Osprey Aviation Elite Units 4 - Lentolaivue 24* (2001) due to new information having since come to light from Russian archives that has allowed a number of damaged claims to be upgraded to confirmed victories.

Key
MHR – Mannerheim Cross
KIA – Killed In Action
KIFA – Killed In Flying Accident
PoW – Prisoner of War

Commonwealth Aces with Buffalo Claims

Name	Service	Unit(s)	Buffalo Claims	Total Claims	Area
G B Fisken	RNZAF	243, 453	6/1/1	11/1/1	Mal
R D Vanderfield	RAAF	453	5/1sh/-	5/1sh/-	Mal
A W B Clare	RAAF	453	5/-/-	5/-/-	Mal
M H Holder	RAF	243	2+3sh/-/2sh	2+3sh/-/2sh	Mal
D J C Pinckney	RAF	67	4/-/1	7/3/3	Bur
B S Wipiti	RNZAF	243	3+1sh/-/-	3+3sh/-/-	Mal
E E G Kuhn*	RNZAF	488	3?/-/-	5?/-/-	Mal
G A Williams*	RNZAF	67	1+1sh/2/3	3+1sh/2/4	Bur
F J Howell	RAF	243	1/-/-	7+3sh/2/2+1sh	Mal

Note
* – those pilots with less than five victories are shown because of their inclusion in *Aces High* or *Those Other Eagles*, where there may be doubt as to their actual scores

Commonwealth Aces that flew the Buffalo

Name	Service	Unit(s)	Total Claims	Area
R A Brabner	RNVR	805	5+1sh/1/1	Med
R E P Brooker	RAF	AHQ	8/2/1	Mal
W M Churchill	RAF	71	4+3sh/-/-	UK
W G Clouston	RAF	488	9+3sh/1+1sh/1sh	Mal
M B Czernin Count	RAF	146	13+5sh/3+1sh/3+2sh	Ind
H J Everard	RCAF	151 OTU	5+1sh/3/3	Ind
J N Mackenzie	RAF	488	8+2sh/2/2	Mal
T A Vigors	RAF	243, 453	6/6/3+2sh	Mal

Notable non-Ace Commonwealth Buffalo Pilots

Name	Service	Unit(s)	Buffalo Claims	Total Claims	Area
M J F Baldwin	RAF	243	2/-/-	2/-/-	Mal
C V Bargh	RNZAF	67	2/2/-	3/2/-	Bur
G R Board	RAAF	453	2+1sh/-/-	2+1sh/-/-	Mal
G L Bonham	RNZAF	243	1/-/1	1/-/1+5 V1s	Mal
M Garden	RAF	243	4/1/1+1sh	4/1/1+1sh	Mal
K Gorringe	RAAF	453	2/1/-	2/1/-	Mal
B A Grace	RAAF	453	2+1sh/-/1	2+1sh/-/1	Mal
H H Griffiths	RAAF	453	2/-/-	2/-/-	Mal
W J Harper	RAF	453	-3/1+1sh/1		Mal
L A Keith	RN	805	-1+2sh/-/2		Med
J R Kinninmont	RAAF	21, 453	2/1/3	2/1/3	Mal
C T Kronk	RNZAF	243, 453	1+1sh/4+1sh/-	1+1sh/4+1sh/-	Mal
M N Read	RAAF	453	3+1sh/-/-	3+1sh/-/-	Mal
N C Sharp	RNZAF	488	2/1/1	3/1/1	Mal
J W Sleigh	RN	804	-1+1sh/-/1sh		UK
D M Sproule	RAAF	21, 25	1/-/-	2/-/-	Mal
R A Weber	RNZAF	243, 453	1sh/-/-	2+1sh/1/-	Mal
J S Wigglesworth	RAF	67	-/1/-	2+2sh/2/-	Bur

Key
Ind – India
Mal – Malaya
Bur – Burma
Med – Mediterranean
UK – United Kingdom

US Navy and Marine Corps Aces that flew the F2A (selective list)

Name	Service	F2A Claims	Total Claims	Area
G Boyington	USMC	-	-	24/4/-	P*
E L Feightner	USN	-	-	9/2/1	T
D Gordon	USN	-	-	5/1/2	T
W A Haas	USN	-	-	4+2sh/-/-	T
H H Hills	USN	-	-	5/1/0	T
C M Kunz	USMC	2/-/-	8/-/-	P
E H O'Hare	USN	-	-	7/1/0	P*
J S Thach	USN	-	-	6/1/0	P*

Key
P – Pacific
T – Training,
* – pre-war

Notable Dutch Brewster B-339 Pilots

Name	Service	Unit	Buffalo Claims	Total Claims	Area
J P van Helsdingen	NEIA	2-VlG-V	3/-/-	3/-/-	M/E
A G Diebel	NEIA	2-VlG-V	3/-/-	3/-/-	M/E
G M Bruggink	NEIA	2-VlG-V	2/-/-	2/-/-	M/E
A A M van Rest	NEIA	1-VlG-V	2/-/-	2/-/-	E

Key
M/E – Malaya/East Indies
E – East Indies

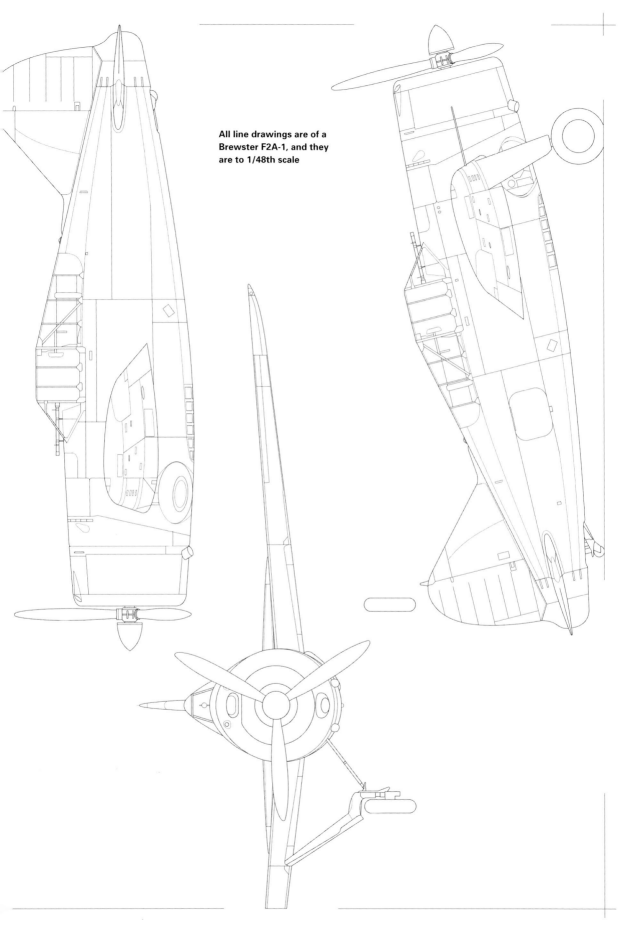

All line drawings are of a
Brewster F2A-1, and they
are to 1/48th scale

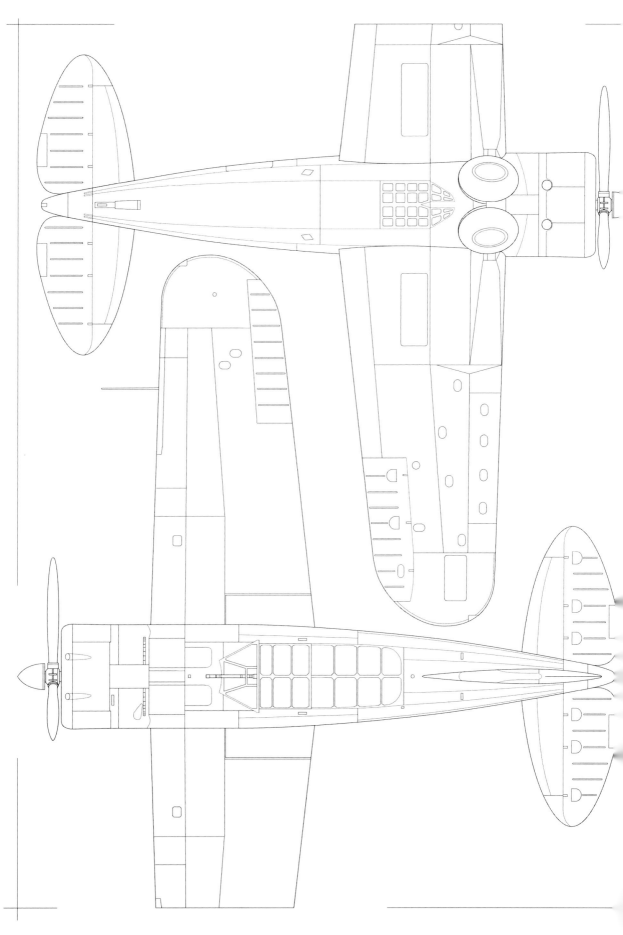

1

F2A-1 BuNo 1393/3-F-13 of VF-3, flown by Lt John S Thach, USS *Saratoga* (CV-3), 19 March 1940

Lt 'Jimmy' Thach was a regular Naval officer and pilot with VF-3 aboard *Saratoga* during the spring of 1940. On 19 March he was flying this aircraft when he had the misfortune to tip it onto its nose when landing back aboard the aircraft carrier – the damage was soon repaired. Later that summer and autumn, BuNo 1393 was regularly flown by another pilot who was destined to achieve great fame, Ens 'Butch' O'Hare, who would receive the Medal of Honour. Like Thach, he too was to become an ace during the early months of the war with Japan. Assigned to the *Saratoga* Air Group, this aircraft is finished in a typically colourful pre-war US Navy scheme.

2

Buffalo I AS419 of 805 NAS, flown by Lt R A Brabner, Maleme, Crete, 19 March 1941

Three examples of the portly Buffalo were used by 805 NAS for the defence of the strategically important island of Crete. One of the pilots assigned to the unit at this time was Lt Rupert Brabner, who had been elected as a Member of Parliament in 1939. He scrambled in this aircraft after Italian bombers on 19 March 1941, but the fighter developed engine trouble and he returned to Maleme. Unfortunately, a power loss on final approach caused him to land short of the runway and the Buffalo overturned. Luckily, the aircraft's anti-roll bar worked and the MP escaped unharmed. Brabner made his first claim during the battle for Crete, and went on to achieve 'acedom' flying Sea Hurricanes with 801 NAS during the epic convoy battles of 1942.

3

Buffalo I W8182/WP-Q of No 243 Sqn, flown by Sgt G B Fisken, Kallang, Singapore, June 1941

W8182 was delivered to No 243 Sqn in Singapore on 20 May 1941 and was flight-tested by the man destined to become the most successful Allied Buffalo pilot, New Zealander Sgt Geoff Fisken. The 23-year-old former shepherd flew this aircraft a number of times, although it had but a brief career with No 243 Sqn. On 23 July, whilst being flown by Plt Off Don Oakden, it suffered an engine failure and was ditched into the sea some seven miles northeast of Kallang. The wreckage was salvaged a few days later.

4

Brewster Model 239 BW-361/'White 8' of 1/LLv 24, flown by 1Lt Joel Savonen, Mikkeli, July 1941

Joel Savonen had flown Gladiators with LLv 26 during the Winter War, although he did not make any claims with the biplane fighter. Savonen served with 1/LLv 24 throughout the Continuation War, except for a three-month spell as an instructor at the Air Fighting School in early 1943. As one of the senior reserve officers, he was deputy flight leader of 1/LLv 24 for a long period of time. Savonen ultimately scored a total of nine confirmed aerial victories, all bar one of them with the Brewster Model 239 – his first claim came in BW-361 on 16 July 1941.

5

Brewster Model 239 BW-366/'Orange 6' of 3/LLv 24, flown by Capt Jorma Karhunen, Lappeenranta, August 1941

'Joppe' Karhunen had 'made ace' flying the D.XXI during the Winter War in 1939-40, and on mobilisation for the Continuation War he was promoted to flight leader of 3/LLv 24. The latter would ultimately emerge as the most successful flight in the whole of Fighter Command. Karhunen flew this aircraft until he became CO of LeLv 24 on 1 June 1943 – he would lead the unit until war's end. Awarded the highly coveted Mannerheim Cross on 8 September 1942, Karhunen scored the bulk of his 25.5 Brewster victories in this aircraft.

6

Brewster Model 239 BW-383/'Black 7' of 4/LLv 24, flown by SSgt Martti Alho, Rantasalmi, August 1941

Martti Alho also flew in the Winter War, claiming 1.5 victories with the D.XXI. He was a long time member of 4/LLv 24, and scored all of his 13.5 Brewster victories at the controls of BW-383. On 15 February 1943 Alho's flight was redesignated 2/LeLv 24, and he was promoted to warrant officer on 16 May 1943 at the age of 24. Alho lost his life in a flying accident on 5 June when he crashed on take-off in the 'wooden wing', Shvetsov M-63-powered, Brewster BW-392.

7

Brewster Model 239 BW-380/'Black 1' of LLv 24, flown by Maj Gustaf Magnusson, Rantasalmi, August 1941

'Eka' Magnusson commanded LLv 24 during the Winter War, when he claimed four victories. He led the unit during the Continuation War until 27 May 1943, when he was posted to command LeR 3 (to which LeLv 24 was assigned). Magnusson scored his fifth kill – in this aircraft – on 8 July 1941, so becoming an ace. Both a very capable fighter pilot and an astute leader of men, Magnusson was awarded the Mannerheim Cross on 26 June 1944. By war's end fighters under his command had claimed 1100 victories for the loss of just 53 aircraft.

8

Brewster Model 239 BW-379/'Orange 9' of 3/LLv 24, flown by 1Lt Pekka Kokko, Immola, September 1941

Pekka Kokko, who had claimed 3.5 victories in the Winter War, served as deputy leader of 3/LLv 24 from the start of the Continuation War. His double victory claim on 29 June 1941 in this very aircraft brought him ace status. Assigned BW-379 for much of his time with LLv 24, Kokko applied his Christian name, *Pekka*, to the nose of the machine – a rare instance of an individual marking on a Finnish fighter. Having claimed ten victories with the Brewster, Kokko left the unit to become a test pilot on 24 November 1941. He perished in a flying accident on 19 February 1944.

9

Buffalo I W8198/NF-U of No 488 Sqn RNZAF, flown by Flt Lt J N Mackenzie, Kallang, Singapore, October 1941-January 1942

When No 488 Sqn RNZAF formed in September 1941, one of its flight commanders was Flt Lt John Mackenzie, a New

Zealander in the RAF and grandson of a former Prime Minister of New Zealand. This aircraft was delivered to the squadron on 8 October and first flown by Mackenzie on the 25th. He flew it occasionally thereafter, and on operations against the Japanese at least three times on 20 and 21 January 1942. On the 18th Sgt Jim MacIntosh used W8198 to probably destroy two A6Ms, commenting favourably on the fighter's manoeuvrability. It was destroyed at Kallang by G3M 'Nell' bombers of the Genzan Kokutai during a raid on 22 January.

10
Buffalo I AN196/WP-W of No 243 Sqn, flown by Flg Off M H Holder, Kota Bharu, Malaya, 8 December 1941
At the time of the first Japanese attacks on Malaya, No 243 Sqn was maintaining a detachment of two aircraft, including AN196, at Kota Bharu in the north of the country. At 0630 hrs on 8 December both aircraft (with Flg Off 'Blondie' Holder at the controls of AN196) took off and flew a strafing attack against Japanese landing barges spotted on the Kelantan River. This was the Buffalo's first action against the Japanese. Holder's aircraft was hit by ground fire, and it suffered further damage when it struck an abandoned Hudson upon landing back at base. AN196 was left behind when Kota Bharu was evacuated later that same day. Holder went on to become one of just four Allied pilots to achieve ace status in the Buffalo.

11
Buffalo I W8157/TD-M of No 453 Sqn RAAF, flown by Flt Lt T A Vigors, Sembawang, Singapore, 10 December 1941
When the Japanese attacked HMS *Prince of Wales* and HMS *Repulse* on 10 December, Buffaloes from No 453 Sqn, led by Battle of Britain ace Flt Lt Tim Vigors in this aircraft, arrived just in time to see the last of the mighty vessels slip beneath the waves. W8157 next saw action on 15 January when Flt Lt 'Congo' Kinninmont, originally of No 21 Sqn RAAF, probably destroyed a Ki-48 – the first of his six Buffalo claims. Four days later he was again flying it when, over Malacca, he shot down a Ki-51 'Sonia' and a Ki-43 'Oscar'.

12
Buffalo I AN185/TD-V of No 453 Sqn RAAF, flown by Plt Off R D Vanderfield, Ipoh, Malaya, 13 December 1941
AN185 was regularly flown by future ace Flt Lt Doug Vanderfield who, on 13 December, headed up to Butterworth in it along with two other Buffaloes. However, on landing, a Japanese raid appeared and all three fighters took off immediately. Vanderfield, in AN185, quickly discovered that he was unable to raise his undercarriage! Unperturbed, he dived on the intruding Japanese bombers and sent down two twin-engined Ki-48 'Lilys' and a single-engined Ki-51, thus beginning his road to 'acedom'. Vanderfield continued to occasionally fly this aircraft, including on 9 January when he got stuck in the mud at Kluang taxiing out on a strafing sortie to Kuantan, and for the last time on the 19th when he escorted some Wirraways to Muar.

13
Buffalo I W8209/TD-F of No 453 Sqn RAAF, flown by Sgt M N Read, Ipoh, Malaya, December 1941
This Buffalo was delivered to No 453 Sqn on 23 September 1941, and on 10 December it was flown by future ace Doug

Vanderfield on a patrol off Kuantan. Three days later Sgt Mal Read flew the fighter to Butterworth, where he followed Vanderfield off to engage an incoming raid. His he was credited with the destruction of two Ki-51s in the wake of this action. Read was at W8209's controls once again on the 22nd when Buffaloes had their first major engagement with JAAF Ki-43s, one of which collided with the promising Read, who was killed.

14
Buffalo I W8245/RD-D of No 67 Sqn, flown by Sgt G A Williams, Mingaladon, Burma, 23 December 1941
When the first JAAF raid on Rangoon occurred on 23 December 1941, 23-year-old Kiwi Sgt Gordon 'Willie' Williams was already on patrol at the controls of this aircraft. As the escorting fighters became engaged with his wingman, Williams saw an opportunity to attack the bombers. Diving on the formation of Ki-21s, he was subsequently credited with shooting one of them down, probably destroying another and damaging four more. Williams was in action again (this time in W8228) during the next raid two days later, when he shared in the destruction of a bomber and claimed a fighter as a probable. He later flew Hurricanes with No 67 Sqn and made ten claims in total, including at least 3.5 destroyed. Like Williams, W8245 also survived the Burma debacle and was evacuated to India, where it was employed as a fighter trainer.

15
Buffalo I W8243/RD-B of No 67 Sqn, flown by Sgt C V Bargh, Mingaladon, Burma, 23 December 1941
Also flown by a young New Zealander in the form of Sgt 'Ketchil' Bargh, W8243 engaged the enemy over Rangoon on 23 December 1941 too. On sighting the huge Japanese formation, Ketchil was promptly engaged by the omnipotent Ki-27 escort that gave him a torrid time. He managed to evade them, however, and upon sighting the bomber formation Bargh was able to deliver a telling attack that destroyed one Ki-21 and probably destroyed another. In all, he made five claims against the Japanese (four of them with the Buffalo), including three destroyed. W8243 was one of the few Buffaloes to reach India, where it served until being struck off charge in late 1943.

16
Brewster Model 239 BW-351/'White 4' of 2/LLv 24, flown by WO Yrjö Turkka, Kontupohja, January 1942
'Pappa' Turkka was one of the squadron's old hands, having finished the Winter War only one shared victory short of 'acedom'. The two SB bombers that he destroyed with BW-351 on 25 June 1941 made him an ace. Turkka flew this aircraft for the first six months of the Continuation War until it was damaged on 10 January 1942. Subsequently assigned BW-357, he eventually scored ten victories with the Brewster and finished the war with 17.5 kills to his name.

17
Buffalo I W8138/NF-O of No 488 Sqn RNZAF, flown by Plt Off N C Sharp, Kallang, Singapore, January 1942
W8138 was the regular mount of 21-year-old Noel Sharp, who personalised it with a very distinctive Chinese dragon marking. In early January 1942 he was temporarily attached to No 243 Sqn for combat operations, although he retained his aircraft.

Flying it on 12 January in his first combat, Sharp probably destroyed a Japanese fighter. In another action the following day, again in this aircraft, he went one better and downed a Ki-27, while on the 18th he claimed his second victory by shooting down an A6M Zero-sen of the 22nd Air Flotilla. However, Sharp had most of his rudder shot away in the process and was also wounded, although he was able to safely land the crippled Buffalo. His colourful mount was repaired and later handed to No 453 Sqn. Sharp achieved further successes flying Hurricanes with No 605 Sqn, but was later killed in Java.

18
Brewster B-339C B-3100 of 2-VIG-V ML-KNIL, flown by Lt A G Deibel, Kallang, Singapore, 12 January 1942
The Brewster-equipped 2nd Squadron of the 5th Fighter Group (2-VIG-V), Netherlands East Indies Air Force, had a Java rhinoceros as its unit badge, whilst the aircraft of the 1st Flight featured a red spinner and a broad white band forward of the vertical tail. Lt August Deibel belonged to this unit, and he was one of the pilots detached to Singapore to support the RAF. He was flying this aircraft on 12 January when, in the early afternoon, he took off to intercept a raid escorted by Ki-27 'Nate' fighters. In the subsequent dogfight four JAAF fighters were claimed shot down, two of them by August Deibel. He was in turn slightly wounded and forced to bail out of his crippled machine.

19
Buffalo I W8139/WP-B of No 243 Sqn, flown by Flt Lt M Garden, Kallang, Singapore, 12/13 January 1942
W8139 was one of the first aircraft delivered to No 243 Sqn, being delivered the day after the unit formed on 12 March 1941. Remaining with the squadron into 1942, it was flown by a number of pilots, including Battle of Britain ace Flt Lt Tim Vigors. Indeed, he suffered a mid-air collision in it on 2 April 1941 when, despite losing his propeller, he landed safely. W8139 later saw action in the ill-fated defence of Singapore, and on 12 January 1942 it was flown by Flt Lt Mowbray Garden in a head-on attack against a formation of JAAF aircraft in misty conditions. Garden was credited with a pair of Ki-27s destroyed and another as a probable – his first victories. However, one came so close that its aerial dented W8139's wing! The following day Garden used the fighter to help Sgt R A Weber down an A6M. Initially claimed as damaged, their victim may well have been PO1c Hiroshi Suyama of the 22nd Air Flotilla, who was lost that morning.

20
Buffalo I W8193/WP-V of No 243 Sqn, flown by Sqn Ldr F J Howell, Kallang, Singapore, 16 January 1942
This aircraft was the regular mount of No 243 Sqn's CO, Sqn Ldr Frank Howell, who led an abortive scramble in it on Christmas Day 1941. He had better luck on 16 January 1942 when the enemy sent over a pair of C5Ms on a reconnaissance mission. Howell (once again in W8193) led off a section and soon spotted one of the enemy aircraft over Johore. He succeeded in shooting it down with just ten rounds, the C5M's starboard wing detaching in flight. This aircraft gave Howell his tenth, and final, victory, and his only success with the Buffalo. The following day W8193 was in the thick of the action again when Flg Off 'Blondie' Holder got in amongst a formation of

bombers and destroyed a Ki-48, shared in the destruction of two more and claimed a fifth as a probable. These three kills took him to 'acedom'.

21
Buffalo I AN180/GA-B of No 21/453 Sqn RAAF, flown by Sgt A W Clare, Sembawang, Singapore, December 1941-January 1942
This aircraft was delivered to No 21 Sqn on 19 November 1941 and coded GA-B. After the debacle in northern Malaya, aircraft were often flown by pilots from other units, and on 17 December Sgt Bill Collyer of No 453 Sqn was flying it when he probably destroyed a Ki-43. Three days later, both RAAF units were amalgamated as No 21/453 Sqn, and on 17 January GA-B (recorded in error as AN160) was flown by Sgt Alf Clare when he downed a Ki-27 'Nate' and then shared in the destruction of a 'Navy Type 0' fighter. The latter, however, was almost certainly the 64th Sentai Ki-43 flown by Lt Rokuz Kato, who was killed. His demise was Alf Clare's fifth success, thus making him the first Allied pilot to achieve 'acedom' with the Buffalo.

22
Buffalo I W8147/WP-O of No 243 Sqn, flown by Sgt B S Wipiti, Kallang, Singapore, 21 January 1942
This aircraft was the regular mount of the most successful Allied Buffalo pilot, Kiwi Sgt Geoff Fisken, who claimed five of his victories with it, including two 'Nells' on 17 January. Four days later another future ace, Maori Sgt Bert Wipiti, was flying W8147 when he was engaged by some Ki-43s. One of the Japanese fighters went into a dive and shed both of its wings after it was attacked by Wipiti. During a subsequent sortie that same day, Fisken was credited with his fifth victory, but on 18 January the RAF's most successful individual Buffalo was lost when Sgt Vin Arthur was shot down and killed whilst attacking 'Nell' bombers.

23
Brewster Model 239 BW-368/'Orange 1' of 3/LLv 24, flown by Sgt Nils Katajainen, Kondupoga, March 1942
'Nipa' Katajainen first saw combat at the very beginning of the Continuation War, and duly became the first all-Brewster ace on 12 August 1941 when he claimed two I-153s in this very aircraft. He then spent seven months flying anti-submarine missions in captured SB bombers until eventually securing a transfer back to 3/LeLv 24 on 7 April 1943. Katajainen scored 17.5 of his 34.5 victories with the Brewster (8.5 of them in BW-368), these kills earning him the Mannerheim Cross on 21 December 1944.

24
Brewster Model 239 BW-384/'Orange 3' of 2/LeLv 24, flown by 2Lt Lauri Nissinen, Tiiksjärvi, May 1942
'Lapra' Nissinen was originally a member of 3/LLv 24 until he was posted to the 2nd Flight on 28 January 1942. He became the second member of his squadron to gain 20 victories in the Continuation War, being awarded the Mannerheim Cross for his successes on 5 July 1942. Sent to the cadet academy shortly thereafter to train as an officer, Nissinen returned to the 1st Flight 12 months later as its commander. Nissinen's Brewster score was 22.5, 12.5 of which he claimed in BW-384 – including three Hurricanes destroyed on 6 April 1942.

He would subsequently lose his life in combat on 17 June 1944 while flying a Bf 109G, his tally having by then reached 32.5.

25

F2A-3P Buffalo BuNo 01512/MF-17 of VMF-221, flown by 2Lt Charles M Kunz, Midway Island, 4 June 1942

The only US ace to claim victories in the F2A was 2Lt Charles Kunz, who flew this aircraft during VMF-221's gallant, though ill-fated, interception of the incoming Japanese strike on Midway on 4 June 1942. He flew his first familiarisation flight with VMF-221 on 30 March, and performed regular tactical training sorties over the next two months. On the morning of 4 June Kunz scrambled in this aircraft as part of the third division and engaged a Japanese dive-bomber group. Quickly downing two D3A 'Vals', he was getting himself into position for a further attack when he was engaged by Zero-sen escorts. Their fire hit his aircraft and wounded him in the head. Dazed, Kunz managed to avoid further damage and land safely back on Midway. This highly eventful sortie proved to be his final flight in an F2A. Kunz later added six more victories to his tally flying F4F-4 Wildcats with VMF 224 over Guadalcanal in September-October 1942.

26

Brewster Model 239 BW-352/'White 2' of 2/LeLv 24, flown by MSgt Eero Kinnunen, Tiiksjärvi, June 1942

Having claimed 3.5 victories with the D.XXI in the Winter War, 'Lekkeri' Kinnunen became an ace on 25 June 1941 – the first day of the Continuation War – after claiming 4.5 SB bombers destroyed in this aircraft during the course of two missions. Continuing to score steadily, primarily in BW-352, Kinnunen ultimately claimed 19 victories with the Brewster. Having transferred to 3/LeLv 24 in October 1942, he was the youngest (aged 25) warrant officer in the air arm at the time of his death on 21 April 1943 – Kinnunen was shot down by an La-5 of 4th GIAP whilst at the controls of BW-352. The black 'Farting Elk' on the tailfin was the 2nd Flight emblem.

27

Brewster Model 239 BW-372/'White 5' of 2/LeLv 24, flown by 1Lt Lauri Ohukainen, Tiiksjärvi, June 1942

'Lasse' Ohukainen joined LLv 24 as a cadet officer in September 1941 and became deputy flight leader of the 2nd Flight on 10 January 1942. Achieving ace status on the first day of the following month, Ohukainen started flying BW-372 in late March. He used the fighter to claim seven Lend-Lease Hurricanes destroyed between 30 March and 25 June 1942. On the latter date Ohukainen was himself downed in this aircraft by a Hurricane from 152nd IAP, the ace ditching his burning fighter in a small lake behind enemy lines before escaping to safety on foot. Shortly after returning to his unit, Ohukainen changed his family name to Pekuri. On 16 June 1944, while serving as leader of 1/HLeLv 34, he was shot down again (in Bf 109G MT-420). This time, however, the 18.5-kill ace was captured.

28

Brewster Model 239 BW-393/'White 7' of 1/LeLv 24, flown by Capt Eino Luukkanen, Römpötti, October 1942

'Eikka' Luukkanen had led 3/LLv 24 during the Winter War, claiming 2.5 victories. The experience he gained during this conflict was put to good use in the first 18 months of the Continuation War, when he commanded 1/LLv 24 and achieved 14.5 kills with the Brewster. Although he claimed victories in six different Model 239s, Luukkanen enjoyed the bulk of his success in BW-393, claiming his final seven Brewster kills with it. Shortly before being promoted to major, and being given command of LeLv 30, he applied beer bottle labels on both sides of BW-393's fin to denote all of his victories up to this point. CO of Bf 109G-equipped HLeLv 34 from March 1943, Luukkanen was awarded the Mannerheim Cross on 18 June 1944 and finished the war with 54 victories to his name.

29

Brewster Model 239 BW-367/'Black 6' of 4/LeLv 24, flown by 1Lt Erik Teromaa, Suulajärvi, November 1942

Erik Teromaa served with 4/LLv 24 from August 1941 through to 30 May 1944, claiming eight Brewster victories during that time – four in BW-367. Posted to lead 1/HLeLv 26 (then also flying Brewsters), he added four more kills to his tally between 9 and 18 June 1944. After a seven-week posting to HLeLv 24, where he flew Bf 109Gs (and claimed six kills), Teromaa returned to 2/HLeLv 26 as its flight leader on 20 August 1944. Flying BW-361, Teromaa scored the last aerial victory credited to the Finnish Air Force when he downed a German Ju 87D over Lapland on 3 October 1944. This kill took Teromaa's final tally to 19.

30

Brewster Model 239 BW-364/'Orange 4' of 3/LeLv 24, flown by WO Ilmari Juutilainen, Suulajärvi, February 1943

A Winter War veteran with two and one shared victories to his name, 'Illu' Juutilainen became the first pilot in LLv 24 to score 20 Continuation War kills on 28 March 1942. This achievement brought him the Mannerheim Cross on 26 April 1942 – again a first for LLv 24. Juutilainen had BW-364 assigned to him until February 1943, and he claimed 28 out of his 34 Brewster victories with it (including three triple kills in a day) between 9 July 1941 and 22 November 1942. He received his second Mannerheim Cross on 28 June 1944 whilst flying Bf 109Gs, and had built up a tally of 94 confirmed aerial victories by war's end, making Juutilainen the top scoring fighter pilot of the Finnish Air Force.

31

Brewster Model 239 BW-370/'Black 4' of 2/LeLv 24, flown by 1Lt Aulis Lumme, Suulajärvi, May 1943

Reservist officer Aulis Lumme was posted to 4/LLv 24 shortly after the start of the Continuation War, and he became an ace on 22 November 1942 flying this particular aircraft. On 15 February 1943 the 4th Flight was redesignated 2/LeLv 24, and Lumme commanded it between May and September 1943. He finished the war with a score of 16.5 kills, 11.5 of which were claimed flying the Brewster (4.5 in BW-370). The white Osprey with a fish in its talons was initially the 4th Flight's emblem, and it was transferred to the 2nd Flight when the former was redesignated.

32

Brewster Model 239 BW-393/'Orange 9' of 3/LeLv 24, flown by 1Lt Hans Wind, Suulajärvi September 1943

'Hasse' Wind flew this aircraft from November 1942 through to May 1944, at first with 1/LeLv 24 and from June 1943 as the leader of the 3rd Flight. The most successful Brewster exponent of them all, he claimed a total of 39 aerial victories with the fighter, 26 of them in BW-393. Wind's Brewster score included a single mission tally of four kills and two triple victory hauls. He received the Mannerheim Cross on 31 July 1943 and again on 28 June 1944, when his score stood at 75. Flying a Bf 109G, Wind claimed five kills that day prior to being badly wounded. He spent the rest of the war in hospital recovering from his injuries.

Back Cover
Brewster Model 239 BW-355/'Orange 7' of 3/HLeLv 24, flown by SSgt Leo Ahokas, Suulajärvi, April 1944
Leo Ahokas served with 3/LLv 24 from August 1941 until war's end. He 'made ace' fairly late in the conflict, claiming his fifth kill on 20 May 1943. Ahokas frequently flew BW-355, which was marked with the victory tally of the aircraft rather than the pilot. Its inscription beneath the cockpit dated back to 1940, when well known Finnish company Nokia Oy donated sufficient funds to pay for the acquisition of the aircraft

COLOUR SECTION

1
Brewster BW-356 is seen here at Tiiksjärvi airfield, in southern Viena, in September 1942. Assigned to 2/LeLv 24, the fighter had been flown by 18-victory ace 1Lt Lauri Ohukainen earlier in the year (*Pauli Ervi*)

2
BW-372 of 2/LeLv 24 was put on display in the Finnish Air Force Museum in 2009. On 26 June 1942, while being flown by ace 1Lt Lauri Ohukainen (who claimed seven kills with the fighter), BW-372 was shot down in flames by a Hurricane of 152nd IAP. Ohukainen ditched the aeroplane into a small freshwater lake north of Sesozero, where it remained for 56 years. Eventually located by a team of warbird enthusiasts from Finland and Russia for the National Museum of Naval Aviation (NMNA) in Pensacola, Florida, the Brewster was recovered from the lake in August 1998. After spending a number of years in storage, BW-372 was loaned by the NMNA to the Finnish Air Force Museum and put on display after it had been cleaned up and the damage inflicted on the wreck during the recovery operation repaired (*Esa Muikku*)

ACKNOWLEDGEMENTS

The authors wish to record their gratitude to the following Brewster pilots who have given of their time in answering queries and presenting accounts for inclusion within this volume – the late Gp Capt G B M Bell OBE, Rear Adm E L Feightner US Navy, AVM L W G Gill DSO, Cdr Don Gordon US Navy, the late Col Jorma Karhunen MHR, Mrs Grace Kunz (widow of the late Col Charles Kunz US Marine Corps), the late Maj Gen Gustaf Magnusson MHR, the late Col Lauri Pekuri and the late Cdr John Sykes RN. Finally, thank you also to Ms Lena M Kaljot of the US Marine Corps Historical Centre and Cdr Peter Mersky US Navy.

BIBLIOGRAPHY

Bennett, John, *Defeat to Victory*, RAAF Museum, 1994

Brook W H, *Demon to Vampire*, Demonvamp, 1986

Bowyer, Michael, *Fighting Colours*, PSL, 1969 & 1975

Caidin, Martin, *Ragged, Rugged Warriors*, E P Dutton, 1966

Cull, Brian et al, *Buffalos over Singapore*, Grub St, 2003

Dean, H R, *RNZAF in South East Asia*, Dept of Internal Affairs, 1966

Ewing, Steve and Lundstrom, John, *Fateful Rendezvous*, Naval Institute Press, 1997

Flintham, Vic and Thomas, Andrew, *Combat Codes*, Airlife, 2003 and 2008

Francis, Neil, *Ketchil*, Wairarapa Archive, 2005

Gamble, Bruce, *Black Sheep One*, Ballantyne, 2000

Halley, James, *Squadrons of the RAF and Commonwealth*, Air Britain, 1988

Herrington, John, *Australians in the War 1939-45*, *Series 3 Volume 3*, Halstead Press, 1962

Jefford, Wg Cdr C G, *RAF Squadrons*, Airlife, 1988 and 2001

Keskinen, Kalevi and Stenman, Kari, *Aerial Victories Vols 1 and 2*, K Stenman, 2006

Keskinen, Kalevi and Stenman Kari, *Brewster Model 239 Vols 1 and 2*, K Stenman, 2005

Juutilainen, E I, *Double Fighter Knight*, Apali, 1996

Luukkanen, E A, *Fighter over Finland*, Macdonald, 1963

Rawlings, John D R, *Fighter Squadrons of the RAF*, Macdonald, 1969

Richards, Denis, *RAF Official History 1939-45, Parts 2 and 3*, HMSO, 1954

Rudge, Chris, *Air-to-Air*, Adventure Air, 2003

Shores, Christopher, Cull, Brian and Malizia, Nicola, *Air War for Yugoslavia, Greece & Crete*, Grub Street, 1987

Shores, Christopher and Cull, Brian, *Bloody Shambles Vol 1*, Grub Street, 1991

Shores, Christopher and Cull, Brian, *Bloody Shambles Vol 2*, Grub Street, 1993

Shores, Christopher, *Those Other Eagles*, Grub Street, 2004

Shores, Christopher and Williams, Clive, *Aces High Vol 1*, Grub Street, 1994

Shores, Christopher, *Aces High Vol 2*, Grub Street, 1999

Stenman, Kari and Keskinen, Kalevi, *Finnish Fighter Aces*, Osprey, 1998

Stenman, Kari and Keskinen, Kalevi, *Lentolaivue 24*, Osprey, 2001

Thomas, J Helsdon, *Wings over Burma*, Merlin, 1984 and 1991

Vigors, Tim, *Life's Too Short to Cry*, Grub Street, 2006

References to illustration captions are shown in **bold**. Plates are prefixed pl and followed by the page number in brackets where its caption appears.

Ahola, Capt Leo 11, 21, 22, 23
Alho, MSgt Martti **15**, 23, **34**, pl**56**(91)
Allshorn, Sqn Ldr, RAF 43, 45
Alvesalo, 1Lt Uolevi 26
Antilla, Sgt Kalevi 27
Armistead, Capt Kirk, USMC 79, 80bis, **81**
Arthur, Sgt Vin, RNZAF 65, 93
Avikainen, Sgt Onni 39

Baldwin, Sgt M J F 'Ginger', RAF 64, 65bis
Bargh, Sgt Vic 'Ketchil', RNZAF 43, pl**58**(92) **68**, 69–71, 69bis, **70**, **71**, 73–4, **76**, 76bis, 77
Beable, Sgt E H, RAF 69
Bell, Sqn Ldr Gerald, RAF 42
Benjamins, Lt P, NEIA 67
Bingham-Wallis, Flg Off Peter, RAF **68**, 69, 72, 73bis, 75, 76
Board, Sgt Greg, RAAF 48bis
Bonham, Plt Off G L 'Snowy', RNZAF 54, 64bis, 67
Brabner, Lt Rupert, RNVR **9**, 9, pl**55**(91)
Brandt, Sqn Ldr Jack, RAF 69bis, 73, 74, 75, 76, 77bis
Brewer, Flg Off Paul, RAF 75bis, 77
Brewster B-339B: Belgian AF, NX56B 7–8, **8**; French AF 8
Brewster B-339C/D: Netherlands East Indies AF 8, 49, 54, 67; B-396 67; B-3100 **51**, 51, pl**59**(93); B-3107 67
Brewster Buffalo:
   RAAF: A51-10 82; A51-15 **82**; AN172/GA-S **53**; AN180/GA-B **44**, 53, pl**60**(93); AN185/TD-V **cover**(4), **46**, pl**57**(92); AN196/WP-W **44**bis, 44-5, pl**57**(92); AN210/TD-J **46**; AN213/TD-Z **43**
   RAF 8, 42; W8134/WP-M **67**; W8138/NF-O 51, **52**bis, pl**59**(92-3); W8139/WP-B **42**, **50**, pl**59**(93); W8142/WP-N **42**; W8144/RD-C 73; W8147/WP-O pl**60**(93); W8157/TD-M **45**, pl**57**(92); W8182/WP-Q pl**55**(91); W8193/WP-V 53, pl**59**(93); W8198/NF-U **50**; W8203/ 75; W8209/TD-F pl**58**(92); W8213/ 76; W8227/GA-E **45**; W8229/ 75; W8239/RD-A **72**, 75; W8243/RD-B pl**58**(92) **70**, 70; W8245/RD-D pl**58**(92) **70**, 72, **77**; W8250/ 77;
   RN: AS419 9, 9, pl**55**(91); AS420 9; AX813 9; AX814 9
Brewster F2A-1: US Navy 6–7; BuNo 1393 '3-F-13' **7**, pl**55**(91) see also Brewster Model 239, Finnish AF
Brewster F2A-2, US Navy, BuNo 1412 '2-F-7' **7**, 7
Brewster F2A-3 7, 78, **81**, 84; US Navy, BuNo 01512/ MF-17 pl**61**(94) **80**, 80; USMC: 2-MF-13 79; BuNo 01537/221-MF-1 79; BuNo 01550 79 see also Brewster B-439
Brewster Model 239: Finnish AF 10, 10–11, 84
   BW-351 12, **22**, 31, pl**58**(92); BW-352 **2-3**, **12**, 12, 23, **32**, **34**, 34, 36, pl**61**(94); BW-353 13, **21**; BW-354 11, **25**, 25, 36; BW-355 **31**, **back cover**(95); BW-356 **25**, 40, pl**63**(95); BW-357 **13**, **28**, **41**, 92; BW-359 23; BW-361 **15**, pl**55**(91) **83**, 83; BW-362 24; BW-364 15-16, **21**, **24**, **29**bis, 30, **37**, pl**62**(94); BW-365 16; BW-366 **19**, 21, **30**, pl**56**(91); BW-367 **33**, pl**62**(94); BW-368 **14**, 15, **24**, 24, pl**60**(93); BW-370 **38**, pl**62**(94); BW-372 23, **27**, 27, pl**61**(94), pl**63**(95); BW-373 29; BW-375 20; BW-376 **20**, 20, 31, 32; BW-377 **15**, 31, 84; BW-378 **18**, 19, **20**, 29; BW-379 13, **18**, pl**56**(91); BW-380 13, **14**, **37**, 37, pl**56**(91); BW-381 23, 27; BW-382 **19**, 41, 84; BW-383 **15**, 23, pl**56**(91); BW-384 **10**, **23**, 23, pl**60**(93-4); BW-385 21; BW-386 **35**; BW-387 **26**; BW-388 30, 38; BW-390 **26**; BW-393 28-9, 32, **33**, **38**, 38, 40, pl**61**(94), pl**62**(94-5); BW-394 26
Brooker, Sqn Ldr Richard, RAF 49
Bruggink, Sgt Gerardus 'Tub', NEIA 51, 52, 67

Christiansen, Sgt W J, RAF 72, 75
Churchill, Sqn Ldr Walter, RAF 8
Clare, Sgt Alf, RAAF **44**, 48bis, **53**, 53, 54, pl**60**(93)
Clouston, Sqn Ldr Wilf, RAF **43**, 43, 50
Clow, Sgt D L, RNZAF 52
Collyer, Sgt V A 'Bill', RAAF **cover**(4), **44**, 93
Cooper, Plt Off A A, RAF 76
Cox, Plt Off E W, RNZAF 64
Cranstone, Plt Off J M, RNZAF 66
Cutfield, Sgt P T, RAF 77
Czernin, Sqn Ldr Count Manfred, RAF 77

Daly, Sqn Ldr H C N, RAAF 82
Darley, Wg Cdr George, RAF 49
Deibel, Lt August, NEIA **51**, 51, pl**59**(93) 67bis
Dickey, Marine Gunner, USMC 79

Elfving, 1Lt Henrik 21
Elsdon, Sqn Ldr Jimmy, RAF 76
Everard, Flg Off Hedley, RCAF 77

Feightner, Ens E L 'Whitey', USN 78
Finn, Sgt John, RAF 75, 77
Fisken, Sgt Geoff, RNZAF 43, 46, 47, 48, 50-1, 51, 54, pl**55**(91) 65, **66**, 66bis, **67**, 84, 93
Forster, Oberfeldwebel Hermann 9

Garden, Flt Lt Mowbray, RAF 43, 46, 49, **50**, 50, 51, 52, 53, pl**59**(93) 65, 66, 67
Gill, Flt Lt Bill, RAF 68, 77
Ginman, Cpl Curt **17**, 19
Gordon, Ens Don 'Flash', USN 78
Gorringe, Sgt K, RAAF 64
Grace, Flt Lt B A, RAAF 43, 47, 48, 53
Griffiths, Sgt Harry, RAAF 48

Harper, Sqn Ldr W J, RAF **43**, 43, 48, 64
Harrison, Lt Bill, USN 78
Harvey, Lt Cdr Warren, USN 6
Haynes, Capt Robert, USMC 79
Heinonen, Sgt Tauno 23, 36
Helsdingen, Kapt Jacob van, NEIA 49, 51, 52, 67
Hewitt, Sgt E B 'Ted', RAF 74, 77
Hietala, SSgt Oiva 84
Holder, Flg Off 'Blondie', RAF 43, **44**bis, 47, 50, 54, pl**57**(92)
Howell, Sqn Ldr Frank, RAF 43, **49**, 49, 51, 53, pl**59**(93)
Huotari, Sgt Jouko 14, 15, **16**, 24, **29**bis
Hutcheson, Flt Lt John, RAF 43, 51, 64bis, 67

Juurinen, 2Lt Aarno 83
Juutilainen, WO Ilmari 14bis, 15, **16**, **21**, 22-3, **24**, 24, **29**bis, 30, **37**, pl**62**(94)

Karhunen, 1Lt Jorma **10**, 11, 14, 14-15, 15, **16**, 17, 18, 18-19, **19**, 21bis, 23, 24, 28, 29, 29-30, **30**, 30, 31bis, 33, **34**, 34bis, 36, 39, pl**56**(91)
Katajainen, Sgt Nils **14**, 15, **16**, **24**, 24, 29, pl**60**(93)
Kato, Lt Rokuz, JAAF 53, 93
Kato, Maj Tateo, JAAF 48
Kauppinen, 1Lt Osmo 24
Kauppinen, SSgt Viljo 40, **41**
Keith, Lt Lloyd, RN 9
Kinninmont, Flt Lt Jack 'Congo', RAAF **45**, 52–3, **53**, 64bis, 92
Kinnunen, MSgt Eero **12**, 12, 14, **25**, 31, **34**, 34, 36, pl**61**(94)
Kirkman, Flt Lt R A, RAAF 64
Kokko, 1Lt Pekka 12-13, 14, 15, **16**, **18**, 18, 30, pl**56**(91)
Koskela, Sgt Paavo **25**, 25
Kronk, Sgt Charlie, RNZAF **49**, 49–50, 53, 65, 66
Kuhn, Sgt Eddie, RNZAF 50, 52, **54**, 64bis, 67
Kunz, 2Lt Charles M, USMC pl**61**(94) 79, **80**bis, 80–1, **81**

Lambert, Flg Off J F, RAF 71, 74, 77
Lampi, Sgt Heimo 11–12, **25**bis, 25, 41
Leckrone, Plt Off Phil, RAF 8
Lehtiö, Sgt Sulo **25**, 40
Lehto, Sgt Urho 23, **25**
Lilja, Sgt Jouko 38
Lindberg, 2Lt Kim **16**, 35
Lorentz, Col Richard 11
Lumme, Sgt Aulis **22**, 29, 33bis, 35-6, **38**, 38, pl**62**(94)
Luukkanen, Capt Eino **10**, 11, 16, **17**, 19, 19-20, 20, 21, 30-1, **32**, 32, **33**, **38**, pl**61**(94)

McCaul, Maj V J, USMC 79
MacIntosh, Sgt W Jim, RNZAF 52, 92
Mackenzie, Flt Lt John, RAF 43, **48**, **50**, 50bis, pl**57**(91-2) 65
McNabb, Flg Off Ron, RAF 74
Macpherson, Sgt John, RAF 73, 74, 77
Magnusson, Lt Col Gustaf 11, 13, **14**, 21, **34**, 34, 39, pl**56**(91)

Malin, Sgt 19
Matsuura, 2Lt Haruo, JAAF 64
Meharry, Sgt H J, RNZAF 52
Mellin, Cpl Paavo **16**, 18, 24
Milward, Sqn Ldr R A, RAF 42, 69
Mitchell, Plt Off, RAAF 82
Montefiore, Flg Off 'Monty', RAF 46, **82**

Neefus, Capt James L, USMC 79
Nissinen, SSgt Lauri 13, **16**, 17-18, **23**, 23-4, 26, 40-1, pl**60**(93-4)
Nuotio, Lt Col Einar 11

Oakden, Plt Off Don, RNZAF 91
Oelrich, Sgt R R, RAAF 48
O'Hare, Lt(jg) 'Butch', USN **7**, 7, 91
Ohukainen (later Pekuri), 1Lt Lauri 22, **25**, 25, 26bis, **27**, 27, pl**61**(94) 95bis
Oliver, Sgt John B, RNZAF 47, 52

Parks, Maj Floyd B, USMC 79
Parsons, Sgt H W, RAAF 64
Peltola, SSgt Eino 23, **25**
Pinckney, Flt Lt Colin, RAF 42, 69bis, **72**, 72, 73bis, **75**, 75ter, 77bis
Pokela, 1Lt Väinö 23, **25**
Puro, 2Lt Olavi **26**, 37–8
Pyötsiä, WO Viktor **10**, **17**, 19, **20**, 20, **36**

Raito, 2Lt Aarno 29
Read, Sgt Mal, RAAF **cover**(4), 47, 48
Rest, Kapt Andrias van, NEIA 67
Ri, Sgt Maj Kontetu, JAAF 74
Riihikallio, 2Lt E **34**, 35, 36–7
Rutherford, Sgt Ken, RAF 77

Sadler, Sgt E L, RAF 76
Sakuraba, PO2C Yoshihiro, IJNAF 64
Salovaara, 1Lt Martti 41bis
Sandoval, Lt, USMC 80
Sarjamo, 1Lt Urho **15**, **22**, **35**, 37, 40
Sarvanto, 1Lt Jorma **10**, **13**, 34, 36, 38
Savonen, 1Lt Joel 15, 19, **31**, 31, 36, pl**55**(91)
Scheffer, Sgt J F, NEIA 67
Sharp, Flg Off G S, RAF **70**, 72, 77
Sharp, Plt Off Noel, RNZAF 51, **52**, 52, 64bis, 65, 67
Shields, Plt Off R S, RAAF 44, 45
Someya, Lt Masashi, JAAF 74
Sovelius, 1Lt Per-Erik 11, 17, **18**, 19, **20**, 21, 22bis
Stone, Sqn Ldr 'Bunny', RAF 76
Strömberg, 1Lt Georg 15, **16**
Suhonen, 2Lt Väinö 20, 31, **39**
Suyama, PO1c Hiroshi, IJNAF 52, 93
Swarts, Ens F, NEIA 52
Sykes, Sub Lt John, RN 9

Takayama, Lt Takeo, JAAF 48
Teromaa, 1Lt Erik **22**, **33**, 33, pl**62**(94) **83**, 83, 83–4
Thach, Lt John S 'Jimmy', USN **7**, 7, pl**55**(91)
Thomas, Mech J Helsdon 75
Tolonen, Sgt Paavo 32
Törrönen, 1Lt Iikka 17, 22, 25, **34**, 34, 35, 36–7, **37**, 37
Turkka, WO Yrjö **10**, 12, 22, **28**, pl**58**(92)

Vahvelainen, Sgt 19
Vanderfield, Flt Lt Doug, RAAF **cover**(4), 43, **46**, **47**, 47, 48, 52-3, 53, pl**57**(92) 64, 92
Vesa, Sgt Emil **29**bis, 39, 40
Vigors, Flt Lt Tim, RAF **42**, 42-3, **45**, 46, 47, 50, pl**57**(92) 67, 93

Weber, Sgt Rex, RNZAF **50**, 52, 93
White, Capt Phillip R, USMC **81**, 81
Wigglesworth, Flg Off John, RAF 69bis, 71–2, 76, 77
Wilkinson, Flt Lt Royce, RAF 8
Williams, Sgt Gordon 'Willie', RNZAF pl**58**(92) **68**, 69, 69–71, 69bis, **70**, 73bis, 77
Williams, Sqn Ldr F H, RAAF 82
Wind, 1Lt Hans **16**, 19, 20, **22**, 24–5, 28–9, 29–30, 31–2, 33, 35, **38**, 38bis, 39, **40**bis, 40bis, 41
Winston, Robert, Brewster test pilot 11
Wipiti, Sgt Bert, RNZAF 47, **49**, 49, 50, pl**60**(93) 64, 65, 66bis, 67